The First-Time Gardener:
GROWING PLANTS AND FLOWERS

Inspiring | Educating | Creating | Entertaining

Brimming with creative inspiration, how-to projects, and useful information to enrich your everyday life, Quarto Knows is a favorite destination for those pursuing their interests and passions. Visit our site and dig deeper with our books into your area of interest: Quarto Creates, Quarto Cooks, Quarto Homes, Quarto Lives, Quarto Drives, Quarto Explores, Quarto Gifts, or Quarto Kids.

First published in 2021 by Cool Springs Press, an imprint of The Quarto Group,
100 Cummings Center, Suite 265-D, Beverly, MA 01915, USA.
T (978) 282-9590 F (978) 283-2742 QuartoKnows.com

Cool Springs Press titles are also available at discount for retail, wholesale, promotional, and bulk purchase. For details, contact the Special Sales Manager by email at specialsales@quarto.com or by mail at The Quarto Group, Attn: Special Sales Manager, 100 Cummings Center, Suite 265-D, Beverly, MA 01915, USA.

25 24 23 22 21   1 2 3 4 5

ISBN: 978-0-7603-6874-9

Digital edition published in 2021
eISBN: 978-0-7603-6875-6

Library of Congress Cataloging-in-Publication Data available

Design: Amy Sly
Cover Image: Shutterstock
Page Layout: Amy Sly
Photography: Allison McManus
Illustration: Lyn Alice | www.LynAlice.com

Printed in China

The First-Time Gardener:
GROWING PLANTS AND FLOWERS

all the know-how you need
to plant and tend outdoor areas
using eco-friendly methods

sean and allison mcmanus
OF SPOKEN GARDEN

COOL
SPRINGS
PRESS

To all the curious, first-time gardeners out there who wish to cultivate their own garden full of beautiful plants and flowers (and keep them alive)

Contents

Introduction

Close your eyes for a minute and picture this: You walk out to your garden space and notice that a bunch of your annuals need deadheading. You know exactly where to snip off the spent flower blooms, without hurting the plant, so you snip away and toss the spent blooms onto your compost pile. It's going to be a warm day ahead, so you check your full-sun perennials to see if they need extra water. You deep water regularly, but you also know the signs of plant stress due to underwatering. Luckily, you knew to add mulch earlier this year to protect your plants and help them retain more moisture. Next, you inspect your daisies for pest damage and, sadly, the slugs were active overnight—but you know what to do. Last, before you rush off to work, you snip off some zinnias, cosmos, and sunflowers to gift as a cutflower bouquet for a coworker's birthday. You're definitely in your happy place. Your garden is healthy, you feel confident knowing how to care for it, and you're doing your part to help the environment with eco-friendly garden practices. Life is good (daydream ends).

Sounds great, right? Well, guess what? The thrill of growing and caring for your own plants is closer than you think. If you worry that you killed all the flowers you bought

at the garden center or that you're unsure about the difference between mulching or pruning, stop worrying! You're here reading this book because you made the decision to learn how to tend to your garden. Good for you! You're already taking the first step toward becoming a better plant parent. We cannot wait to guide you along this journey!

what does it mean to be a first-time gardener?

Calling yourself a "new gardener" is an honor. And, since this term implies different things, let's start by defining it. If you can answer "yes" to any of the following questions, then you can raise your hand (proudly) and declare yourself a "first-timer":

- Are you excited about tending to flowers so you can watch them bloom and grow (and maybe take pictures of them later)?

- Do you lack confidence in your garden skills, no matter how long you've had a garden?

- Are you a new homeowner who just inherited a garden with no idea how to care for it?

- Do you have a renewed interest in growing your own plants and flowers, just because?

Everyone has to start somewhere, right? Well, we'll let you in on a little gardening secret: All gardeners make mistakes. Even professional gardeners and landscapers make errors. There is no such thing as a *perfect* garden or a *perfect* flower. It just does not exist. You *will* make mistakes, and you *will* kill plants. The good news is that learning through trial and error is one of the best ways to improve your skills. Luckily, plants are pretty resilient, too, so there is that.

why garden care is important and how it affects you

One of the best parts about gardening is the healthy dose of nature therapy you'll receive just by surrounding yourself with the beauty of plants and flowers. Plants offer so many rewarding benefits yet ask for so little in return. By nurturing them with the right amount of water, the correct amount of soil, and the proper sunlight (among many other things), your plants will grow into living, breathing beings. They really are amazing organisms.

Growing plants and flowers is not a new concept. In fact, the art and science of gardening is a passion—and has been—for people all around the world. Plants bring us joy, beauty, and nourishment. In addition, they provide cleaner air, healthier soil, and better water. By cultivating your passion for gardening, you can tap into this pipeline instantly.

eco-friendly gardening and zero waste

In the interest of caring for and protecting plants, people often resort to adding harsh synthetic chemical herbicides or pesticides to their garden hoping to control pests (which kills the good insects, too, by the way), eliminate weeds, or manipulate nature in so many other ways. These chemicals get absorbed into the soil, sucked up by plants, consumed by pollinators, and eventually end up in the food chain. Sounds like a nightmare, right? That's why in this book, you'll learn how to tend to your garden using only eco-friendly methods.

Weaved throughout each chapter are tips you'll learn for sustainable ways to care for your garden, including safe ways to control pests while avoiding the use of toxic substances, zero-waste ideas for your garden debris, eco-friendly tips related to each chapter's topic, and so much more.

As a thank you for letting us teach you, check out the free *First-Time Gardener* Bonus Companion Guide. Dig deeper into each chapter with extra video content, PDF downloads, audio, and more. We hope this is helpful for you along your journey!

spokengarden.com/ftgbonusguide

what you will learn in this book

This book is designed to teach you garden skills from the ground up (pun intended). You'll learn how to care for the whole plant, both above and below ground.

After gaining an understanding of how plants grow and what conditions they need to thrive, you'll learn how to plan out a garden space, fill it with new plants, plant them correctly, and tend to them throughout the year. You'll walk away with great tips for solving garden care problems naturally, dealing with common garden pests (squirrels can be the worst), and a whole lot more. In each chapter, look for actionable callouts with specific information you can apply right away. And last, feel satisfied knowing you'll learn eco-friendly solutions to common garden problems that won't harm you, your family, your pets, pollinators, or the environment.

Remember that daydream from earlier? That really *will* be you.

Are you ready to get started? We're so excited to be your guides as you begin this journey to better garden care!

Understanding the Basics about Plants and Flowers: definitions, concepts, and more

Before you learn about growing plants, tending to your flowers, or eco-friendly garden care methods, it's important to have a basic understanding of plants. Similar to how a seed grows into a seedling, your foundation of plant knowledge will begin with fundamental information, then develop and grow throughout the chapter with each new topic. We are going to break it down, all the way down, to a few important definitions and concepts to get you started. You will learn about the basic parts of a plant, what ingredients a plant needs to grow, where a flower comes from, and how pollinators influence this whole process in your garden. Are you ready? Plant Basics 101 is about to begin!

what makes a plant a plant?

By definition, a flowering plant is a living organism that is made up of leaves, stems, roots, and flowers. While not asking for much in return, they will grow, change, reproduce, and die as long as all of their basic needs are met. It really is not all that different from our basic needs. Think about what you need throughout a day to be healthy. You need air, water, food, shelter, and warmth (and you can probably add sleep and a few other items to that list, too). Well, plants have the same basic needs, plus or minus a few.

Digging in a little deeper into that definition, a plant is a group of cells, tissues, and organs that all work together to emerge and grow to a maturity level where it can ultimately reproduce itself using sunlight, water, temperature, carbon dioxide, and other nutrients. In a perfect world, the plant will stay healthy and continue to grow, flower, and reproduce for as long as it can.

Plants come in all different shapes, sizes, colors, forms, and structures. They can be as small as a tiny clover to as large as a giant redwood tree. Within this variety of plant life, all plants have the same basic needs (as you just learned), grow the same way, and have the same basic plant parts. They may look different from plant to plant, but the parts are all there.

Can you identify the plant parts in this photo yet? Leaves, stems, roots, and flower.

PERENNIALS VS. ANNUALS VS. BIENNIALS

Perennial: A plant that continues to grow and flower from the same roots, crowns, or stems for multiple years. Examples: Shasta daisies, coneflowers, and garden phlox

Annual: A plant that grows and flowers for only one season (year), then does not regrow the next year. In other words, it completes its life cycle in a single year. Examples: cosmos, zinnias, and marigolds

Biennial: A plant that takes two full growing cycles, or years, to flower. They usually die after the second year. Biennials are less common than annuals or perennials. Examples: some types of black-eyed Susans, dianthus, and forget-me-nots

One main difference that separates plants into various groupings is whether they are a perennial, annual, or what is called a "biennial." It is important for you to understand these differences because they will determine how you plant and care for them in the later chapters.

Perennials are plants that grow and flower from the same roots, crowns, or stems from year to year. This means, in general, that these plants never die, similar to the 1985 movie *The Goonies* (and yes, we may have just dated ourselves). If you remember, "Goonies never say die." Well, perennials never say die either—as long as all their needs are met, of course. Perennials have strong roots, and some have strong shoots and even leaves, that will survive through the winter months. Some of them even bloom in the winter. Perennials can be further subdivided into herbaceous or evergreen. Often, gardeners fill their gardens with nothing but perennials because they will return season after season and continue to grow larger each year. There are many examples of perennials that you've probably heard of before, including lavender, hellebores, Shasta daisies, coneflowers, and rhododendrons.

On the other hand, a plant is in the *annual* group if it only grows and flowers within 1 year. This type of plant does not regrow the following year. One and done. Many of the beautiful, flowering plants you see at garden centers each spring and summer are

This lavender plant is a great example of a perennial that comes back year after year.

annuals. This includes cosmos, zinnias, petunias, impatiens, and marigolds, among so many others. Annuals grow and flower very quickly, with a true variety and diversity of flower shapes, colors, sizes, and forms for use in your garden. The shear variety and diversity that annuals can provide your garden is what makes them so desirable even though they grow for only 1 year.

The third kind of plant is called a *biennial*. These are less commonly grown and sold than annuals or perennials, and as a result, are often less understood. Biennials take 2 full years to complete their life cycle. Patience is key when planting biennials. They grow leaves and stems (some just leaves) their first year from spring into the fall in your garden and then go dormant that first winter. The next year they grow up again to then flower and complete their whole life cycle. Sadly, they usually die after they bloom. Luckily, these flowers can also reseed each year, so it seems like they stick around a lot longer than just 2 years. When new seedlings emerge, you just have to remember that that specific plant won't flower until the following year. Examples of biennials include some types of black-eyed Susans, foxgloves, and forget-me-nots.

Cosmos, a popular annual plant, germinates, grows, and flowers in 1 year.

Biennials, like this black-eyed Susan, are less common than annuals and perennials due to their growth cycle taking 2 years.

Not only do plants fall into the category of either perennial, annual, or biennial; there is a lot of variety within these groups as well. Trees are the largest plant member of all, with some species reaching heights of 300 feet (91.4 m) tall but can also be small or what's called dwarf varieties, reaching only 5 feet (1.5 m) at maturity. Trees are perennials that can be either deciduous, meaning they lose all their leaves, or evergreen, which means they do not lose leaves and stay green all year. Examples of deciduous trees are dwarf Japanese maples, dogwoods, weeping cherry, apple trees, and more. Evergreen tree examples that are tall are firs, redwoods, pines, and others that you might visualize when you think of a dense forest. A shrub is a lower-growing plant than a tree, but they also produce woody growth. They, too, have both deciduous and evergreen species.

Vinca or periwinkle is a great groundcover to plant along pathways or to fill open garden bed areas.

Often perennials can be further broken down into either woody perennials or herbaceous. Woody perennial plants develop hard tissues that continue to grow from year to year and grow larger in length or girth or both over time. Herbaceous perennial plants grow from a crown with softer tissue each year with just leaves (hosta) or stems and leaves (Shasta daisy) to then flower. A herbaceous perennial will die back down to the ground surface to then be dormant until it regrows leaves, stems, and flowers the next year.

Other types of plants include groundcovers, ornamental grasses, and vines, to name a

few; and they can also be divided into woody or herbaceous plants. Each type of plant has a unique appearance, shape, and best use in the garden. However, all plants, regardless of their type, have the need to grow and reproduce with the same basic needs and general plant parts.

types of plants and their best uses

Plant Type	Description	Best Uses
Tree	A type of plant with a central trunk, or multiple trunks, ranging in height from 5 to 60+ feet (1.5 to 18.3+ m) tall, and varying in width. Plant can keep or lose leaves each year.	Provide shade, structure, height, depth, fruit, and color. Shade gardens look great planted underneath trees.
Shrub	A type of plant with multiple woody stems ranging in height from 2 to 15+ feet (0.6 to 4.6+ m) tall and varying in width. Plant can keep or lose leaves each year.	Provide shape, color, texture, and interest to a garden with their leaves, stems, and flowers. Also good for adding structure.
Groundcover	A plant that grows low to the ground surface and spreads out with its long stems and sub-stems. Can range in height from a mere inch up to 2+ inches (5+ cm). Plant can keep or lose leaves each year.	Useful for covering large garden bed areas that need color or for suppressing weeds. Also can prevent erosion, provide texture, offer leaf and flower color, or add depth to a garden.
Herb	A plant with edible leaves, flowers, or stems. Can take the form of groundcovers, shrubs, and small trees.	Provide texture, flower color, and fragrance. Can be used in medicine, for cooking, and more. Most are pollinator attractors.
Ornamental Grass	A plant that grows in clumps with multiple, individual leaves growing out from a central crown. The leaves often resemble lawn grass.	Provide texture and color. Blades and flowers have a wavy or feathery motion in the wind.
Vine	A plant that grows in trailing stems along the ground, up trellises, on walls, or on other plants.	Useful for covering trellises, walls, or large areas or creating privacy. Weed suppression is possible, too.
Bulb	A type of plant that grows and reproduces from an underground storage organ. Five types of bulbs exist: true-bulb, tuberous root, tuber, corm, and rhizome.	Provide midwinter, early spring, or summer color, depending on the bulb. Great for grouped plantings along borders, around shrubs, and under deciduous trees.

crash course on plant growth

You may not have direct experience holding a seed in your hand yet, but can you picture one in your mind? Any kind of seed will do—a sunflower seed, a large seed, a small seed. Whatever you picture, just hold that image in your mind for a second. What do you notice about the seed? What questions pop into your mind? Is one of them, "How could this tiny seed possibly grow into a giant plant that produces tons of beautiful flowers?" Well, you would not be the first person to ask that very question. Plants are fascinating, and botanists, horticulturists, and other plant professionals agree as they study, experiment, and create (yes, create) new plants every year from seed or bulb (or cutting). Think of all the beautiful plants you see at a garden center each spring or summer. Most of these plants started from seed, and thinking about how a seed becomes a plant is where you will begin this section on plant growth—with a crash course.

First of all, plants grow in two specific ways: (1) They grow over time, or mature over time; and (2) they grow by size. Really, it is not all that different from how we grow and mature over time. We just end up looking a *little* bit different.

1. PLANTS MATURE OVER TIME

Without getting into too much college-level botany or plant physiology, plants go through cycles of development over time just like we do. They begin as a seed then germinate, and then grow into a seedling, similar to how we grow from seed into a baby being born and then into a toddler. Next, plants grow from their seedling stage into juveniles, similar to human teenagers. Then, plants continue to mature so they can flower and reproduce. Over time (or seasons), plants rely on changes in the environment—like temperature, light levels, and water—to tell them when to start and stop growing and when to flower. With this in mind, a plant's maturity is directly related to its size; and over time, a plant will grow larger. Therefore, in general, the bigger the plant, the older it is. For annual plants, they germinate (are born), grow from a seedling into a full plant (teenager), and flower (reproduce themselves) all in 1 year. Perennials germinate (are born), grow from seedlings to a larger plant (teenager), and then can start to flower anytime between the first year up to 5 years, depending on the specific plant. Then, year after year they continue to grow and flower each year. This continues, if all their needs are met.

Hard to believe this tiny sunflower seedling will grow 5 to 6 feet (1.5 to 1.8 m) tall with a dinner plate–sized flower.

2. PLANTS GROW IN SIZE

As plants continue to grow to maturity, they also grow by size, which is the second type of plant growth. Plants grow up (height or length) and spread out (width). They stretch their stems and roots out as they germinate from seed or from last year's growth of a perennial plant, thus growing taller or longer. By stretching, they continue to grow at the tip of that stem (growing point) where the length of stem behind that growing tip then starts to also grow in girth or diameter. At the same time, plants grow wider as they grow taller until they reach their full maturity. As a side note, when buying plants, it is crucial to know the plant's predicted height and width at maturity so you can plan where to plant it in your landscape. When purchasing plants from a garden center, each plant should have a plant tag with this important information listed. We'll talk more about this in the next chapter.

A good example of plants growing in size is a rhododendron or another shrub that has 1- to 2-year-old wood. You can see that the older wood (or tissue) of that plant is wider than at the plant's currently growing stems. That older wood will continue to grow in girth, and the growing point will continue to grow up until the fall when it begins to go dormant. This can be generally referred to as a plant's "up and out" physical growth. This growth pattern can be observed in both annuals and perennials as they grow.

The "up and out" growth of a plant happens both above and below the ground. Above ground, plants grow from their stems as they reach out longer and longer over time. Below ground, plant roots grow in the same way with a stretching growing tip; and

These black-eyed Susan seedlings are similar to human toddlers in their maturity and growth.

behind that tip, the root grows in diameter. This is why most roots have a tapering look to them as you trace them from their ending tip back toward the plant's root center. Plants also grow out from specific points along those stems, usually where you see a leaf attached to the stem—a kind of sub-stem. This helps the plant increase its overall width, or size; and this is why you see the shape you see of the whole plant. So, not only do individual plant stems grow up and out, but the larger plant itself behaves the same way as it also grows up and out in overall height and width. This is why you see the shape of the whole plant. There are variations of this type of growth as we have described it here, so keep that in mind when observing plant growth anywhere.

Now as the plant grows in length and then in girth, along the stem (above ground) it starts to develop growing points called buds at specific intervals predetermined by the plant's genetics. This is the site where leaves, stems, or flower buds will soon grow. The stems and leaves will grow either before or after a plant has flowered.

HUMAN VS. PLANT GROWTH AND DEVELOPMENT

At each stage of human development in the chart below, there is a complementary stage of development for plants. As you can see, both humans and plants begin as seeds, then grow and develop into their mature selves.

Humans	Plants
Egg (fertilized) and develops before birth	Seed (ready to germinate) and born when it breaks through the soil
Infant baby or toddler	Seedling
Juvenile teenager	Juvenile plant
Adult human (mature in size and reproduction)	Adult plant (mature in size and reproduction)

COSMOS PLANT ANATOMY

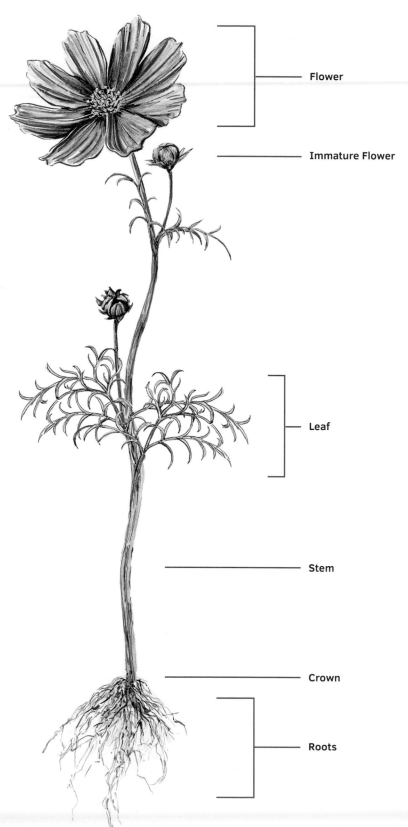

Flower

Immature Flower

Leaf

Stem

Crown

Roots

what parts make up a plant?

Now that you are aware of how plants grow over time and by physical size, let's dive in a bit deeper. You may already know that plants are made up of leaves, stems (shoots), roots, and flowers (or maybe not, and that's okay); but it is helpful to know where each of these parts is located and how they interact. Beginning at the bottom of the plant, plants have roots that take in water and nutrients so the plant can grow. They look almost look like a head of hair, or tiny individual hairs, that grow and branch out into finer, even smaller hairs. Above the plant's roots is the start of the plant stem, or crown, where the roots meet the stem. This is a kind of junction. Moving farther up the plant, the stem grows thicker and provides structure to help the plant grow even more stems, leaves, and flowers. It also helps move water and nutrients to different areas of the plant where they are needed. Growing off the stem are the plant's leaves. They are the plant's power generator, converting sunlight (solar energy) into usable energy for the plant to continue growing more. Also, leaves are the location where plants absorb carbon dioxide and exhale (or push out) oxygen for us to breathe. Moving farther up the plant sits the flower, or reproductive parts where a plant gets its flower fertilized or pollinated so that seeds can develop and spread.

For all these plant parts to grow and develop, they need to take in specific things from their immediate environment and wait for seasonal triggers that happen throughout a year. Plants grow because of these five main ingredients: sunlight, water, carbon dioxide, soil, and temperature. With these ingredients, a plant will take solar energy and convert it into usable energy for its further development.

Sunlight you already know about, but what do water, carbon dioxide, soil, and temperature really contribute to plant growth? Water is important for plant growth to keep plants hydrated and nutrients moving through different "plumbing" tissues. Carbon dioxide is part of the process called photosynthesis, where the plant takes it in to break it down as part of converting sunlight into usable energy. Soil keeps a plant anchored in place and provides a medium for water, nutrients, and air to be taken up by plant roots. And temperature helps to regulate and signal different plant development during seasonal changes, along with water and nutrient availability.

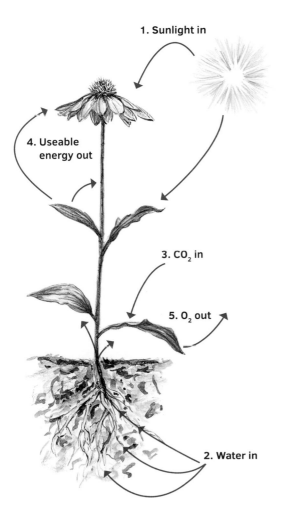

Coneflower photosynthesis

1. Sunlight in

4. Useable energy out

3. CO_2 in

5. O_2 out

2. Water in

Photosynthesis is the process of plants harnessing sunlight to convert it to usable energy to keep growing, developing, and ultimately reproduce or flower. Sunlight is collected by a plant's leaves, where water coming up from the roots of the plant is transported. With the water and the sunlight, the plant leaves also take in carbon dioxide gas bringing all these elements together for the plant to produce usable energy in the form of carbohydrates then to transport it around to the other parts of the plant where it can sustain itself and where it is actively growing. Along with the carbohydrates being an end product of photosynthesis, the plant also pushes oxygen gas out of its leaves into the surrounding air. This ends up being the air we breathe. Pretty cool, right? The process of photosynthesis continues in the plant as long as it has healthy roots, stems, and leaves with as much water and light as it needs.

Roots, on the other hand, generally continue to grow slowly underground throughout most of the year, increasing in both length and in girth. This is the normal pattern for both perennial and biennial plants from month to month and year to year. On the other hand, annual plant roots will also continue to grow, but only during the plants' short life span within that 1 year.

Now that you know how plants generally grow, you need to know what plants need to thrive and grow. They need the right amounts of sunlight and water, along with growing within specific temperature ranges, and in the right soil with the right water drainage.

To go deeper, let's start with knowing plants' need for certain amounts of sunlight and recognize that some plants need more light than others. We know plants need sunlight to convert it into usable energy, but some plants can do this while growing entirely in the shade, in partial shade or sun, or in full sun for a majority of the day. Be aware of this for when we talk about choosing new plants for your garden.

LEVELS OF SUNLIGHT SPECIFIC PLANTS PREFER

Shade-Loving: hosta, vinca, rhododendron, hellebore, ajuga, camellia, aucuba, Skimmia, coleus, and Sarcococca

Partial-Shade-Loving: hosta, hydrangea, Pieris, mahonia, mint, cyclamen, primrose, ajuga

Full-Sun-Loving: black-eyed Susan, crocus, sunflower, zinnia, daffodil, tulip, peony, crocosmia, jasmine, petunia, Shasta daisy, celosia, and lavender

the ingredients that create a plant and help it grow

There are five main inputs that any plant needs to grow and thrive, as you already know. They need light, water, carbon dioxide, soil, and temperature. These can get tricky and vary from region to region. The only constant is carbon dioxide, since there is plenty of it in our atmosphere. You'll find out more about the remaining four factors in the plant hardiness section of this chapter and in the soil section of Chapter 2, but we'd like to briefly discuss them here.

If you have not already noticed, plants react to their surrounding environment. Sunlight, temperature, carbon dioxide, soil, and water (or lack thereof) can force plants to grow, wilt, stand up or lay over, stretch, burn, drown or dry up, change color, and much more. To show the importance of plants reacting to the surrounding environment, you will learn how sunlight, water, soil, and temperature are all essential for a plant to grow and thrive.

SUNLIGHT

Sunlight helps plants convert light energy into usable energy so they can process and consume carbohydrates, minerals, and other nutrients to grow their shoots, roots, leaves, and flowers. If a plant, like lavender or zinnia, needs a full-sun exposure but is planted in a partial-sun location of your garden, then it will not have access to enough light energy to convert to usable energy. It will do its best to keep growing and to flower, but you will generally have longer, weaker stems, fewer leaves, and both smaller and fewer flowers. Until this lavender or zinnia plant gets more sunlight, it will continue to grow like this for the rest of its life. The opposite could happen with a plant that prefers lower light levels, like hellebore or hosta, if it receives too much sunlight in a full-sun location. In this example, the hellebore or hosta can develop discolored or burnt leaves, small flower stems, and few or no flowers. This is why it's important to pay attention to a plant's preferred light level.

WATER

Water is also very important to plants because, just like us humans, they need to have enough water for all their cells, tissues, and organs to grow and thrive. Water needs vary from plant to plant. This really depends on how a plant has evolved to grow in specific water situations. Some plants need very little water to thrive, like many different cacti and succulents. Other plants like to have lots of water all the time. Without getting into too much botany here, each cell, tissue, and organ of a plant keeps an internal pressure that's partially regulated by water (and salts) to stay fully expanded in size and for all the enzymes, nutrients, and biochemistry to take place. Having a plant be optimally hydrated helps it keep turning light energy into usable energy by leaves being fully extended and green, flowers open and the right color, stems and the whole plant upright, and generally keep the plant healthy to ward off any pests and diseases. Think of it this way: We humans have to drink water every day to be healthy, along with consuming energy in the form of food calories. If we don't drink enough water during a day or a few days in a row, we get dehydrated where our blood vessels, tissues, and even organs shrink. Our bodies function less efficiently and become stressed by the lack of water. We become more open and susceptible to diseases and organisms that can hurt or kill us. The lesson here is to keep your plants optimally watered to their preferred moisture levels so they can perform their best.

SOIL

Plants also need soil to stay anchored, along with being able to take up water, nutrients, and air. Yes, I said air because plant roots actually need to breathe. You will learn more about soil in the next chapter, but the basic importance of soil to plants is to anchor them to stand up straight to access sunlight, water, and air and take in nutrients to stay healthy. Soil is exceptionally important for water, but also the right amount of water. Too much or too little can hurt any plant and eventually kill it, so the drainage or movement of water through soil is key here. Drainage of soil is impacted greatly by soil texture, that is, the key makeup of any soil with sand, silt, clay, and organic matter. More on that in Chapter 2, but for now, that is why soil is important for plant growth.

TEMPERATURE

Last on our recipe for plant growth is the importance of temperature. Each plant has a temperature range within which it germinates, grows, and matures each year to eventually flower and complete or continue its growth cycle. As you learned earlier, this could be in 1 year for one plant (annuals) or year after year for other plants (perennials). Temperature directly relates to plant growth and can be thought of in meeting specific degree requirements for different stages of a plant's growth, like seed germination, seedling growth into a larger plant, flowering, and then producing seeds. A great example of this is zinnias or sunflowers. Both are annual plants that require daytime soil temperatures to be continually warm enough to germinate and grow until they flower and produce seeds for the next year. Another example of how temperature controls plant growth is the number of cold winter temperature days some types of flowering bulbs, fruit trees, and certain other plants need before they can grow and flower. If a specific cold temperature is not reached for a continual period of time, these types of plants won't grow or flower (which explains why tulips won't flower in tropical climates—they need winter!).

flower fundamentals

This African daisy shows different flower parts, each with specific functions and bright colors to attract pollinators.

Flowers are amazing in their ability to make us feel, think, smell, and even taste. We as human beings have found numerous ways to use flowers in our everyday lives, from showing appreciation and love, respect, and honor to also putting them in our food and using parts of them to heal and treat different diseases and ailments. You can see these uses of flowers all over the world, and it is extraordinary!

Plants possess a kind of "courting" process wherein they produce flowers to attract pollinators to help with the fertilization in exchange for a nectar reward. The resulting seeds are the next generation and will continue their genetic line into the future. Most plants have evolved to produce flowers to complete their life cycle. And we get to be their stewards as gardeners to help do all this.

In general, flowers grow and mature on stems called a pedicel. At the very end of the pedicel are located the flower sepals or modified petals. They can be green or another color depending on the plant species. Then just above the sepals are the flower petals. The sepals and petals are usually the most colorful part of the flower and are what attract pollinators to the flower. Just above or after the petals is where all the reproductive parts of the flower start.

There are many variations in flower shape along with color. Other parts of a flower include the stamens (male) and the pistil (female). These serve the same function in nearly every flower. Usually the male parts of the flower (the stamens and anthers), where the pollen comes from, is around or close to the female parts (the pistil and ovary), which are usually located in the center of the flower. The pollen needs to go from the male part to the female part for the flower to be pollinated and for the seeds to start to grow in the lower portion of the flower (the ovary). Some plants have flowers that have both male and female parts. Other plants have separate male and female flowers.

Flowers come in many different shapes. Decide what you like in your garden and around your house, and don't be afraid to mix it up. The flower shapes listed in the sidebar "Common Flower Shapes" on page 31 are grouped into three different categories with examples of each type of flower so you can get a sense of their differences and all the variety of flowers that are out there for you to grow.

There are many different uses for flowers in your garden and numerous reasons why you may consider adding certain ones to your own garden, including:

- To attract pollinators

- For continual color interest throughout one season

- For continual color interest from season to season

- Color accents and groupings

- Texture and flow of form from one area to another

- Traffic flow or to direct the eye in a certain direction

- To excite, calm, or inspire

Common Flower Shapes

SHAPE:
ROUND, GLOBE, OR BALL

Allium flowers are a good example of this shape.

Common examples: allium, globe thistle, button bush

SHAPE:
DAISY-LIKE

Gerbera daisy is a good example of a daisy shape.

Common examples: sunflower, cosmos, gerbera, coneflower

SHAPE:
BELL

Campanula is a good example of this shape.

Common examples: campanula, lily-of-the-valley, foxglove

SHAPE:
TRUMPET, TUBULAR, OR FUNNEL

Fuchsia is a good example of this shape.

Common examples: fuchsia, sage, honeysuckle

SHAPE:
CUP

Tulip Is a good example of this shape.

Common examples: tulip, crocus

SHAPE:
SPIKE

Liatris is a good example of this shape.

Common examples: celosia, lavender, liatris, hyacinth

the pollinator connection

Everyone loves pollinators, right? But not everyone understands how they directly contribute to the overall health of your garden or the environment as a whole. Pollinators include bees, wasps, moths, butterflies, dragonflies, birds, other insects, and small critters. They travel from flower to flower feeding on the flower's nectar or pollen. As they visit each flower, they collect pollen and then transfer and deposit that pollen to the next flower. If everything works according to plan, the pollen they spread will fertilize the new plants and help them start to develop and grow seeds. Plants then get to finish their reproductive cycles of growth. The general rule of thumb is that the more pollinators you have in your garden, the healthier your garden must be; otherwise, you wouldn't see the pollinators.

Now pollinators, bless their little hearts, are attracted to various shapes, colors, scents, or sizes of flowers. Flowers have actually evolved to attract specific types of pollinators to their front door so that pollen can be spread.

Bumblebees love flowers like this allium.

The interesting thing is that the function of flowers is to attract pollinators with their colorful and varying petals to spread pollen. As these pollinators visit and move from flower to flower, they spread the pollen of the previous flower to eventually pollinate and fertilize that flower. Once a pollinator—like a bee, butterfly, moth, hummingbird, and many others—has fertilized the flower with pollen, seed production starts and that flower withers so as not to waste plant resources on continuing to flower because the biological need to reproduce is well under way and pollinators are no longer needed.

ATTRACT POLLINATORS
with Specific Flowers

Hummingbirds love flowers that have long-necked trumpet-shaped flowers, like the flowers on this sage plant.

Bumblebees—Shasta daisy, lavender, lupine, campanula, azalea, dahlia, allium

Honeybees—borage, calendula, cosmos, snapdragon, aster

Hummingbirds—fuchsia, sage, crocosmia, lily, lupine, petunia

Butterflies—Shasta daisy, allium, hydrangea, cosmos, African daisy, delphinium, lavender,

Moths—dusty miller, white pansy, Shasta daisy, white petunia, nicotiana

Dragonflies—black-eyed Susan, swamp milkweed, yarrow,

plant hardiness and its importance

It's not only important to know how plants grow, but you also need to know where plants grow and why. Plants will grow in certain climates and regions where temperature extremes (hot and cold), available water and nutrients, and soil structure, along with drainage, are the best for them to grow and reproduce. The ability of a plant to withstand certain temperature extremes is known as its hardiness.

The hardiness of your plants can be thought of in a couple different ways, and you should be familiar with or at least have heard of these. This is so you can understand

how your plants can grow in your local climate under different seasonal conditions. Plant hardiness is generally thought to describe a plant's ability to be cold hardy to your local climate's average lowest temperatures. This is given in a range from highest to lowest. For example, a hosta plant can be cold hardy from –40°F to –35°F (–40°C to –37°C), and a ficus plant is cold hardy from 45°F to 40°F (7°C to 4°C). The difference between the two plants and their temperature ranges is staggering. The hosta grows each year up out of the ground in the spring and summer to then wither back down to the ground, going dormant until the next spring.

above These hosta leaves aren't as hardy as you might think. In the fall, they will die back down to the ground to reemerge the following spring.
opposite Certain plants can withstand different ranges of cold temperatures, including frost and snow.

The ficus only grows above ground, has woody stems, and evolved in warmer climates; it cannot tolerate very cold temperatures.

There are other aspects of plant hardiness that can be thought of more as a plant's ability to tolerate or resist climate and environmental extremes. Depending on where your garden is, you will need plants that aren't just hardy for the coldest local average temperatures but also hardy under conditions of drought, heat, flooding, wind, specific soil, and pests and diseases. Basically, this means that certain plants will only grow in specific locations based on their general hardiness to that location's growing characteristics. If a plant is not hardy to your garden's specific location for seasonal temperature differences, rainfall, sun exposure, soil conditions, and regional pests, then it will eventually die. Therefore, it is especially important to make sure your plant is hardy to your local region's climate. You can read more on this in Chapter 2 on plant hardiness and "Right Plant, Right Place" on page 47.

plant hardiness and seasons

Seasons are one way we track time. We watch the changes in plants when they emerge, grow, flower, and then wither; and we see them start the whole process over the next year. Our seasons are defined by temperatures and the months of the year, whether you live in the northern or southern hemisphere. There are four seasons to each year, and each season is around three months long. The four seasons are generally known as winter, spring, summer, and fall. In temperate climates where seasonal changes are more evident than in tropical climates, winter is generally when many plants are dormant (above ground, anyway) when temperatures are coldest and day lengths are the shortest. Spring is generally when many garden plants start to wake up and begin to either leaf-out, flower, or grow. Summer is generally when plants still grow and show lots of flowers and color. Fall is generally the season of wrapping up flowering and seed production, and it's when plants begin to slow down and begin their dormancy period to last through the coming winter months. Of course, there are certainly plants that begin to flower during fall and continue into the winter

This dianthus plant blooms both in the spring and in the fall.

months, and there are others that produce their seeds in the spring—there are many differences in the plant world. In Chapter 7, we review seasonal garden topics and dive more deeply into what to do and when, so more is to come on the topic of seasonality.

your new knowledge

Your plant knowledge is already growing. With your new understanding of plant growth and the ingredients plants require, you are ready to learn how multiple plants and flowers fit together and coexist in your garden, like a puzzle. In Chapter 2, we will go into further detail about this puzzle while you continue to expand your knowledge. Get ready to learn how to match a plant to your region, find the right location in your garden for that specific plant, and fit that plant to your needs.

KEY TAKEAWAYS FROM THIS CHAPTER

- Plants need the right recipe of temperature, soil, water, air, and sunlight to grow.

- Flowers are the reproductive part of a plant.

- Flowers come in different shapes and colors to attract different pollinators.

- Certain plants are hardy to specific garden conditions in order to thrive and flower.

DIG DEEPER

For your plants to thrive and be healthy, they need to first be hardy to your region. We'll dig deeper into plant hardiness in Chapter 1 of the Bonus Companion Guide so you can better understand how this impacts your plant's overall health. Check it out at spokengarden.com/ftgbonusguide.

chapter

2

The Building Blocks of Your Garden: plant needs, garden layout, and containers

Building your garden knowledge involves more than just learning about what parts make up a plant, how they grow, and what hardiness means. Although these are *crucial* pieces of information, it is not the whole picture. Now, you need to think about how individual plants fit together into a garden space and then coexist with one another. Will they get along? Is one plant going to outgrow another plant? How can you tell?

As you can see, buying plants is just one part of creating your garden. First, you need to know *which* plants to buy. Next, it's important to learn how to choose the correct plants, where to place those plants in your garden, and what kind of soil you might need before planting *anything* (even though you really, really want to). Why? Because certain plants will only grow in certain conditions. Later in the chapter, you will find out how containers are just tiny ecosystems of their own and which plants might be a good fit for your garden containers. It's time to learn how your garden fits together. Let's roll up our sleeves and start building the blocks that will become your garden!

right plant, right place

Before running out and buying a new plant, first, you need to know if it will even grow in your garden. Otherwise, you may end up just wasting a whole bunch of money. Sure, this will take a bit of planning and some research, but it will be worth it in the end.

We would like to introduce you to the concept of "right plant, right place." This old garden phrase explains how choosing plants that are compatible to their location would be best for your garden's health. It is also a key principle of garden design. The first part of the phrase means that the "right plant" will thrive in your garden for cold hardiness in your regional climate. "Right place," the second part of the phrase, refers to a plant having enough room to grow with the proper amount of sun, water, and soil conditions to thrive in a particular location. Simply put, it means that a plant should grow best when given the right conditions with minimal effort or help from you. That being said, selecting plants to add to your own garden is often a delicate balancing act using "right plant, right place." Finding that balance among cold hardiness, space for the plant to grow, the proper sunlight levels, soil, and water needs can be achieved with time and effort.

It seems like a basic concept, but it's often overlooked by professional landscape architects and garden designers. Also, homeowners might add certain plants or flowers because they look pleasing, but these plants may not be right for their climate or necessarily fit together with other plants. You will learn to do otherwise.

Keeping this concept in mind helps you determine how to pick the correct plants from the get-go and where to transplant your current plants if you need to move things around. As part of "right plant, right place," a good way to start thinking about this is how certain plants would need to be grouped together based on their similar water needs.

A very good example of two plants that should not be planted together. This cactus and this lobelia have very different water needs.

For example, drought-tolerant plants, such as lavender, black-eyed Susans, and sedums, all have similar low water needs and would need to be grouped together. On the other hand, plants like Shasta daisies, campanulas, impatiens, and petunias all need regular water and would prefer to be grouped separately from the drought-tolerant plants.

Now, the caveat is that just because those plants have similar water needs doesn't mean they should always be grouped together based on "right plant, right place." It's almost like a puzzle. How big is each plant going to get? How tall? Will some plants shade out other plants? As you can see, it is necessary to further sort within plant groups even though they have similar water needs.

3 steps to choosing the right plants

According to "right plant, right place," begin by learning how to match specific plants to the regional climactic conditions where your garden is located (it is not as hard as it sounds, we promise). Then, you need to find out if the plants you want to add will survive and thrive in your garden with the amount of sunlight, temperature, available water, and soil conditions available there. The last step, which is the easiest, is choosing what plants and flowers you want based on your climate and your garden's available resources. At this point, it's almost time to shop for new plants; but there is one additional piece of information to consider.

Will the plant you want even fit into the space where you want to plant it? You need to know in advance. No, gardeners are not predictors of the future, making guesses about mature plant sizes (well, maybe some of them are); this information is easily available on plant tags or a quick internet search about the plant. Bottom line, you will need to research the plant's full size at maturity. If you don't, you could set yourself up for lots of problems, extra garden care, or pest damage later on (which you'll learn more about in Chapter 6). Once each of the above conditions is met, you and your plant can have your happily ever after. But first, let's go into a bit more detail about "right plant, right place" and how to do all of this. By the way, plan on becoming best friends with the plant tags that come with each new plant you buy. Pro tip: Make sure you save them so you can reference them later if needed.

STEP 1: MATCHING PLANTS TO YOUR REGIONAL CLIMATE

Plants that will thrive and be happiest in your garden will be those that are appropriate for your regional climate. Period. This is according to the average annual temperatures in your area, including extreme cold and extreme hot. That is why this is the very first step of "right plant, right place." Unfortunately, some plants will not grow in your area as much as you want them to. As an extreme example, think about moving from the equator to the North Pole, never able to fully acclimate to the severe, cold temperatures. You would be miserable, right? The same thing happens with plants. If you live in a cold, northern climate, you probably will not want to add plants that are suited to a hot, dry climate. And, if you live in a hot, dry climate, you most likely won't be adding plants that are unsuitable in the heat. Of course, this is all in the most general sense, and there are ways to "cheat" this step—but none that will be suitable to a healthy garden. Bottom line, it is best to match plants suitable to your local climate. Luckily for you, there are tons of beautiful plants that are suited to every climate, so you just need to do a little research.

STEP 2: MATCHING PLANTS TO THE AVAILABLE CONDITIONS IN YOUR GARDEN

Now that your list is narrowed down to plants that will match your climate, you can continue to find the right plants within the next step of "right plant, right place." In this step, you will match plants with the resources you have available in your garden, including available sunlight, water, soil, and temperature. Again, the goal is to find the best fit and further narrow down your list of plant options to fit your garden puzzle.

Sunlight

If you remember from Chapter 1, a plant needs a particular amount of sunlight to convert into usable energy. Now, your goal is to group multiple plants together into your garden. First, plants need to be matched according to their own sunlight needs. In addition, they also need to be placed in the correct spot for maximum sun exposure and duration of sunlight. This means that plants that have similar needs need to be grouped together. For example, plants that need full sun should

Unfortunately, this lavender plant is not receiving enough sunlight and is planted in the wrong soil.

Lavender will thrive and live its best life when planted in the right place and in the right soil.

all be placed in an area that receives full sun. Plants that are shade loving need to coexist in an area that receives full shade. It is all about grouping "like with like." Sounds easy enough, right? Well, it begins to get a little tricky.

For example, a lavender plant and a lily both need a certain amount of sunlight to survive. The lavender plant thrives in full sunlight all day to be healthy; however, the lily is perfectly fine with full sun for only part of the day and actually prefers mostly partial-shade conditions. For this reason, the lavender and the lily need to be grouped separately with other plants that share their similar needs. The question is, how do you know how much sunlight certain areas of your garden receive? It is time to nerd out for a bit and talk about the sunlight tracking over your garden.

First, find out in which cardinal direction your garden faces and for how long. Cardinal directions are the four points on a compass: north, south, east, and west. These directions are important because the rising and setting of the sun are used as reference points. And you need to know this so you can plan your garden according to the direction it faces, how much sunlight it will receive, and for how long. More pieces of the puzzle to figure out. Building on the previous example with the lavender and the lily, if you want to add full-sun plants, like lavender, they need to be placed in an area that receives at least six or more hours of sunlight a day. Otherwise, they probably will not live very long. On the other hand, plants that thrive in partial shade can, hypothetically, be grouped together because they seek partial shade. In the next chapter, you will go outside and find the cardinal direction for your garden space; but for now, you just need to be aware of the importance. The best news is that there are plenty of plants to choose from if your garden happens to be in mostly shade, mostly sun, or even a mix of both throughout the day. Of course, this is just an example, and plants that grow successfully in one garden may not survive in another garden due to so many other factors, including their soil.

Soil

Sure, sunlight is super important, but so is your garden's soil. Without soil, specifically, the right soil texture, plants would be malnourished, thirsty, and unable to support their own weight, and struggle to reach the sun. This would be really bad. By the way, there are entire specialists within the horticulture profession that study nothing but soil science. We won't go that deep into it, so don't worry; but you do need a basic understanding of soil.

Like you learned in Chapter 1, plants need soil; and certain plants need certain types of soil. Some soils drain water quickly, and others drain slowly. Some soils are full of nutrient-rich, organic material; other soils are not. As part of "right plant, right place," you need to group plants according to the type of soil they prefer. This is where things begin to get a little trickier in your garden. You will learn a whole lot more about soil in the upcoming chapters.

Water

To live their best life, different plants have different water needs. Some plants prefer drought-tolerant conditions, or even the extreme of very little water, for prolonged periods of time. Other plants require lots of water and can never get enough. When choosing plants for your garden, part of "right plant, right place" is to group plants together that have similar water needs. This means that plants that require regular amounts of water want to hang out in the same area of your garden together. Plants that do not require as much water, as a group, should hang out in a different area of your garden. If they mix together, the results could be devastating for the surrounding plants. Even more pieces of the puzzle are coming together.

In addition, pairing a plant's water needs with the plant's soil preferences is key because different soil textures lead to varying amounts of drainage. In this case, a plant like lavender which prefers fast, well-draining soil should never touch a clay-based soil (too poor drainage) and never group together with plants that prefer lots of water. Each plant has an optimal zone of soil texture and water conditions and will thrive when all of these conditions are met.

This daylily loves its home under this deciduous tree planted near other plants with the same water, sun, and soil needs.

Some plants adapt to multiple water conditions, and others cannot. This means that some plants can tolerate a little too much water once in a while or a little bit of drought once in a while. Other plants cannot handle these levels of water extremes and could be more susceptible to disease, plant rot, or death. For example, lavender, iris, and various ferns, along with maple and birch trees, have a higher level of water tolerance if this was the only factor determining their survival (which, as you know, it is not). Plants that have a limited or low tolerance for changing water conditions and extremes are hydrangea, hosta, primrose, sages, and roses. They like what they like, and they don't want to change. It is a fine balance, and it boils down to knowing your plant's needs and grouping plants accordingly.

Temperature

Speaking of change, plants need to be able to tolerate temperature ranges in your local area once in a while, from coldest to hottest. This is similar to, but different than, matching plants to your overall climate as in the very first step of "right plant, right place."

How cold or warm it is during different times of year in your garden and the surrounding region of where you live has a huge impact on the plants you can have and grow in your garden. Not only are the extreme lows and highs important to note, but also the average seasonal temperatures. This can influence how your plants grow, their overall health, and their interactions with the surrounding environment. Of course, when extremely low temperatures suddenly occur, they catch us off guard. The same thing happens to plants. For us, we can literally stand up and move ourselves to a warmer location that is more hospitable, but plants cannot. They must remain in the same location regardless of extreme temperature shifts (plus, how weird would it be if plants suddenly grew legs and walked away?). The same is true when unusually high temperatures occur. Most plants can tolerate extreme temperatures for a bit but not indefinitely. They attempt to find the best balance so that all of their needs are met.

MATCHING PLANTS TO YOUR OWN PREFERENCES

After realizing that some of your dream plants may not even grow in your garden, you may be feeling a bit crushed. However, know this: There are many plants to choose from that grow and thrive in just about every climate, every type of soil, every water condition, and every temperature. That means, you still have a lot of choices to make! This is the fun part!

For example, you might need a plant to grow low and spread over an area to eliminate weeds. Or, maybe you wish to enhance the texture of your garden, add colorful flowering plants, or attract pollinators. Here are other reasons why gardeners might choose specific plants:

• For disease or insect resistance

• For height differences between plants

• To have continuous flowers during different times of year

• For ease of care

• To encourage pollinators

• To have more cut flowers to bring into your home

What color plants and flowers do you prefer? What kind of garden do you want to grow? What is your desired level of garden care (meaning, how much time do you want to spend in your garden tending to it)? Make sure to consider these questions before buying any new plants.

"RIGHT PLANT, RIGHT PLACE" CHEAT SHEET

Sunlight: Plants will need full or partial sun or partial to full shade.

Soil: Plants require optimum sandy, silty, or clay-based soil for their survival with either a high, neutral, or low pH (acidity).

Water: Plants require regular, moderate, or low water to thrive in a garden.

Cold hardiness (or temperature hardiness): This the lowest temperature at which a plant can survive without significant damage to its leaves, stems, buds, or roots.

Space: Each plant needs a specific amount of growing space to reach their mature size.

When choosing plants for your garden, consider how they could adapt to freak temperature swings. Think about the coldest temperature they might be able to tolerate to continue to thrive in your garden. Even if you are unsure, research various government or private organizations online. Often, many have developed systems to categorize and group plants into low-temperature tolerance areas.

STEP 3: DETERMINING THE SPACING OF NEW PLANTS IN YOUR GARDEN

Humans are competitive by nature. As much as we hate to admit it, it is true. Plants are no different. The closer that plants are placed in relation to each other, the higher the competition will be. Therefore, building on the concept of "right plant, right place," you also need to consider plant spacing and layout in your garden.

Plants interact in their garden environment wherever they are located, whether in large garden beds or in containers. And the amount of space a plant is allowed to grow into can quickly become a problem if not enough of that space is available. It comes down to the difference between the size of plants when they are immature versus mature. Unfortunately, this is a step many gardeners overlook. The problem is, you need to understand a plant's full size at maturity and leave enough space for that plant to eventually grow into as its final home. For example, a mature Shasta daisy plant could span 3 to 4 feet (0.9 to 1.2 m) or more in width (and in height). It would be a shame if another plant was placed too close, thus eliminating the chance for the

A good example of correct spacing with these ornamental grasses, hydrangeas, and false dracaenas.

These plants are growing into each other because they were not planted with the correct spacing in mind.

Shasta daisy plant to grow to its full potential. Often, new gardeners will add plants to their garden without considering how big these plants will be at their mature size. These closely spaced plants, whether in a garden bed or a container, will grow into each other and compete for water, soil, nutrients, sunlight, and more.

Often, gardeners aim for instant gratification in their garden. We see this a lot, actually, where new plants are spaced really close together to create an instantly lush garden that is full of color. Unfortunately, this method of "cheating" to create a fully mature garden from the beginning leads to numerous problems in the future. Simple planning would have avoided this whole scenario.

When these dense plantings occur, plants inevitably grow into each other—and fast—which creates competition for sunlight due to overlapping branches and leaves. In addition, plants vie for water and nutrients in the soil, which causes them to keep outgrowing each other at a faster pace. The more these plants need to keep hydrated and grow more leaves, the faster they will use and consume that water and those nutrients. Next, watering times would have to increase, along with more compost or other natural fertilizers to keep the competing plants healthy. This creates stress that is completely unnecessary and can lead to bigger problems such as lack of plant nutrition, dehydration, pest damage, or disease taking advantage of any stressed plants. So, not only is sunlight a spacing concern, but also available water and nutrients being taken from a finite soil space with finite inputs. What a mess!

The opposite of dense plantings are sparse plantings. This is where plants are spaced too far away from each other, creating open garden bed gaps. You might think, "This is great!" Any plant will have more than enough room to grow as wide and as tall as it wants, and they will generally not shade each other out or compete for water and nutrients. Everything will be perfect! Well, we hate to tell you, but NO. Everything will not be perfect. In this situation, these plants for sure will have plenty of room to grow and spread, but there is also opportunity for weed seeds or invasive plants to spread in these open areas. These faster-growing, more aggressive plants will now compete with all your plants. This turns us back to the original problem of competition for

As you can see here, these plants have way too much space that can create future problems with weeds.

water, nutrients, and available sun. Not only do you have to worry about not enough growing space, nutrients, and water for your plants again; but now you have to physically remove each weed plant from your garden—and this will be on a recurring basis, as most weeds don't go away after one removal.

The overarching idea here is to properly place plants according to their needed mature growth size. You will be able to find this out on the plant pot tag when you buy each plant at your local nursery, or you can research and find this information online fairly quickly form reputable sources.

Our advice is to make your plant list and research all plant needs for sun, water, soil, and temperature needs before you go to your local nursery. Also, sketch out a planting plan of where each plant will be placed in your garden.

garden layout considerations

Now we are going to talk about your garden's layout. Yes! This is the fun stuff.

There is only so much planting space available for new plants in most gardens, and only so many plants can fit into any given area. How many depends on each plant's mature height and width. If we think about a sample garden that's 25 square feet (2.3 m2) (5 feet [1.5 m] long and 5 feet [1.5 m] wide, a perfect square shape) in which we'd like to plant English lavender, sage, and Shasta daisies. How do we know how many of each plant will fit in that space? The easiest way to do this is to sketch out this 25 square foot (2.3 m2) area on graph paper so each square equals 1 square foot (0.1 m2). You can then count five squares down and five squares across and draw your square-shaped garden bed. (If your bed isn't perfectly square, adjust your sketch accordingly.) Then, determine the mature size of the English lavender, sage, and Shasta daisy plants. Each grow about 2 to 3 square feet (0.2 to 0.3 m2) across when mature. That means you could fit roughly three or four each of sage and lavender plants, along with six or seven Shasta daisy plants, in this 25 square foot (2.3 m2) bed. This is a really basic example, but it gives you an idea of what is possible.

The plants in your garden should not have to compete against each other for light, nutrients, soil, or water. All you need to do is correctly plant them according to their mature height and width. It seems easy enough, but many gardeners forget this crucial step because, as humans, we default to the quick wins and instant gratification of wanting immediate color and texture. However, by taking the time to properly plan out your garden and space plants correctly, your garden will be healthier and happier in the long run.

soil and other modifications

Dirt, full of particles of all shapes and sizes, is the growing medium for each of your flowers, shrubs, trees, and every other form of plant life (including the weeds). This dirt, or soil, is a complex structure made of different materials, each of which is essential to the health and stability of all your garden plants.

Want to know (another) gardening secret? Soil can be modified, or amended, to fit your needs. Yes, you read that correctly. Soil is the one element of "right plant, right place" that you can "fix" if you need to. Since soil is a natural anchor for your plants that stabilizes them and gives them access to water, nutrients, and air (for their roots to breathe), it has to be just right to accommodate the plant's needs. And this is a great gardening hack that professional landscapers and designers use because it is fairly easy to do. So, for now, let's break through the soil, so to speak, and discuss what's going on under the surface. (By the way, you will actually do this in the next chapter!)

Soil is composed of three different particle textures that combine together. In order of size from largest particle to smallest are sand, silt, and then clay. Depending on their combination within your soil, these particles directly impact how much water, air, and nutrients are available in your soil for plants to use.

DESIGNING GARDENS WITH SPECIFIC PLANTS

Certain plants can be used for specific reasons within your garden, leading to possible design ideas for you to consider. Here are some common plants gardeners add to their garden designs for these popular uses:

- To add privacy: English laurel, boxwood, or holly

- To encourage more pollinators: borage, daisies, milkweeds, native plants

- For groundcovers: vinca, ivy, ajuga

- To help control weeds: vinca, ivy, or ajuga

- To add fine-textured foliage: lavender, ornamental grasses, daylilies

- To add bold-textured foliage: hosta, cannas, elephant ears

sandy soil

silty soil

clay-based soil

You can think about soil in these terms: The more space that exists between soil particles, the faster water will move and drain through that soil, and the more air pockets there will be as well. The opposite is true of smaller-spaced particles: The less space, or tighter, it is between soil particles, the slower the water will move through, and the less air will be available to plant roots. Sand, which is the largest particle of the three, has the largest pore spaces for air and water to move through. Therefore, this particle has the lowest actual surface area for water or nutrients to adhere to. Clay, the smallest particle, has the smallest pore spaces for air and water to move through, holds on tightly to water and nutrients, and has the highest surface area of all the soil types. Since clay-based soils hold on so tightly to water, this is one of the main reasons why flooding happens due to slow drainage. And with soil, it is all about drainage. How quickly water moves through your soil, based on the type of soil texture you have, can either help or hinder a plant's growth and development. The wrong soil texture can even lead to plant death. That is why it is extremely important to know your soil's texture before adding plants to the area. The great news is (notice how we always end on a positive?), you can improve your soil's texture by amending it. You can actually build better soil!

Now, if you were to mix clay soil with sandy soil and mix them only in a planting hole of a new plant where the clay was around the plant roots and the surrounding soil was mostly only sand, you would have great drainage outside of the planting hole in the sandy soil. In the planting hole, however, where it's full of clay-based soil, there would be little to no drainage and possible flooding. Also, water would move through the planting hole very slowly with clay-based soil into the adjacent sandy soil because of the difference in pore size from clay to sand or small (tightly held water) to large (loosely held water) soil particle sizes.

Some plants are more adaptable to different soil types than others. There is a good chance you won't have to modify or change the soil for these plants. Other plants are more particular about the type of soil they grow in (think of cacti and how they grow in sandy soils). In this case, there is a good chance you will have to modify or change the soil for more finicky plants to thrive in your garden. We'll talk more about how and why to do this in the next chapter.

Here is a good example of all three soil textures separated into layers, from top to bottom: clay, silt, and sand.

BEFORE YOU BUY PLANTS, REMEMBER TO FOLLOW THESE STEPS

1. First, research information about each plant, including plant hardiness and climatic needs based on "right plant, right place."

2. Group plants together by their needs using "right plant, right place":
   a. Cold hardiness/climate
   b. Sun
   c. Water
   d. Soil

3. Consider the size of a plant at maturity.

4. Amend/change your garden soil, if needed.

thinking about container design

Your plant puzzle is coming together. You now know how to match plants to your climate's hardiness, available sunlight, water, and more as related to "right plant, right place." Also, you know how to change (ahem, cheat) with your soil to fit your plants' needs. Now, take this whole concept and shrink it. This is how you should think about designing your containers. They offer a much smaller space with even more limited resources.

What is a container? Also referred to as a pot, it is a small contained garden with its own ecosystem—a mini garden if you will. This miniature garden needs more attention than an in-ground garden because it only has a finite amount of soil, water, air, or nutrients to offer the plants you place in it. Your regular garden beds can draw air, water, and even a small amount of nutrients from the surrounding soil if needed, but a container cannot. What you put into a container in terms of water and nutrients (usually in the form of fertilizers or compost) is what is available for the plants. Therefore, the type of soil, available sunlight, temperature, and amount of water (including how it drains) is extremely important to the survival of the plants growing there. Think of it this way: The less you plan and the less intentional you are in planting the right plants in a container

There are many sizes and shapes of containers available for you to choose from.

Notice the difference in sizes and shapes between these containers full of flowering plants.

to fit all these requirements, the more care, watering, and time you will have to put into keeping these plants alive, also, the more problems you will have with insects, disease, and more. Don't get us wrong, we love planting in containers! However, as you can see, you need to be thoughtful when designing them. Luckily for you, there are numerous books devoted to container gardening, but we will touch on the basics of container garden planting and care later in this book.

To further elaborate, soil is a big deal in your containers. It must provide the basic functions of anchoring, providing water, nutrients, and air as well as helping regulate temperatures around plant roots. Drainage is also a large part of your plant's health in container soil. It must drain fast enough not to drown plant roots, but also not so fast that water and nutrients are unavailable for any plant to consume.

Most container-loving plants will thrive in two specific soils: potting soil and a topsoil mix. Potting soil is generally a man-made medium consisting of various proportions of peat moss, perlite, and bark (or another kind of organic matter). Over time, the nursery and plant industry has found that many plants find this potting mix of soil (well, it's not true natural soil but man-made) suitable for most plants that can grow in a container. The topsoil for containers is usually a mix of various proportions of sand, clay, and compost or other organic material. Either of these two "soils" works well for container gardening because each one provides all the same basic functions as natural soil but in a finite ecosystem. In addition, most plants that grow well in containers are adaptable to different growing conditions of temperature, soil, water, light, and minimal or very little growing space. This is great news because this means you have more options to create garden containers than you might have thought possible.

A simple container option can include filling your container with only one type of plant, or a mono planting, like you see here with these primroses.

ECO-FRIENDLY TIP:
PLANTS WANT TO LIVE THEIR BEST LIFE

The center piece in this container, a calla lily, adds height and interest while surrounded by petunias, begonias, and calibrachoa.

Since you now have a better understanding of "right plant, right place," you may have discovered that some plants in your garden are planted in the wrong location and could be happier somewhere else better suited to their needs. Instead of ripping them out and tossing them in the compost bin, find them a new home where they can live their best life. This could be a location somewhere else in your garden or in someone else's garden. Another option is to transplant these plants to a container that you can move to find just the right spot.

what's next?

Now that you know that the right plant must be chosen for the right place, the importance of soils and plant spacing, you are ready to take stock of what you already possibly have in your own garden. In the next chapter, you are going to take an inventory of what is in your garden. You cannot logically begin building anything without first understanding what you already have, so get ready to get to know your garden space a little bit more.

KEY TAKEAWAYS FROM THIS CHAPTER:

- The right plant needs to be planted in the right place.

- Make sure to give your plants enough space to grow into for their mature size.

- One thing you can change for your plant's health is the soil it grows in.

- A container is a small garden with its own ecosystem.

DIG DEEPER

To learn even more about different plants you can add to your containers by season, visit our Bonus Companion Guide to dig deeper into your plant choices. Check it out in Chapter 2 at spokengarden.com/ftgbonusguide.

chapter 3

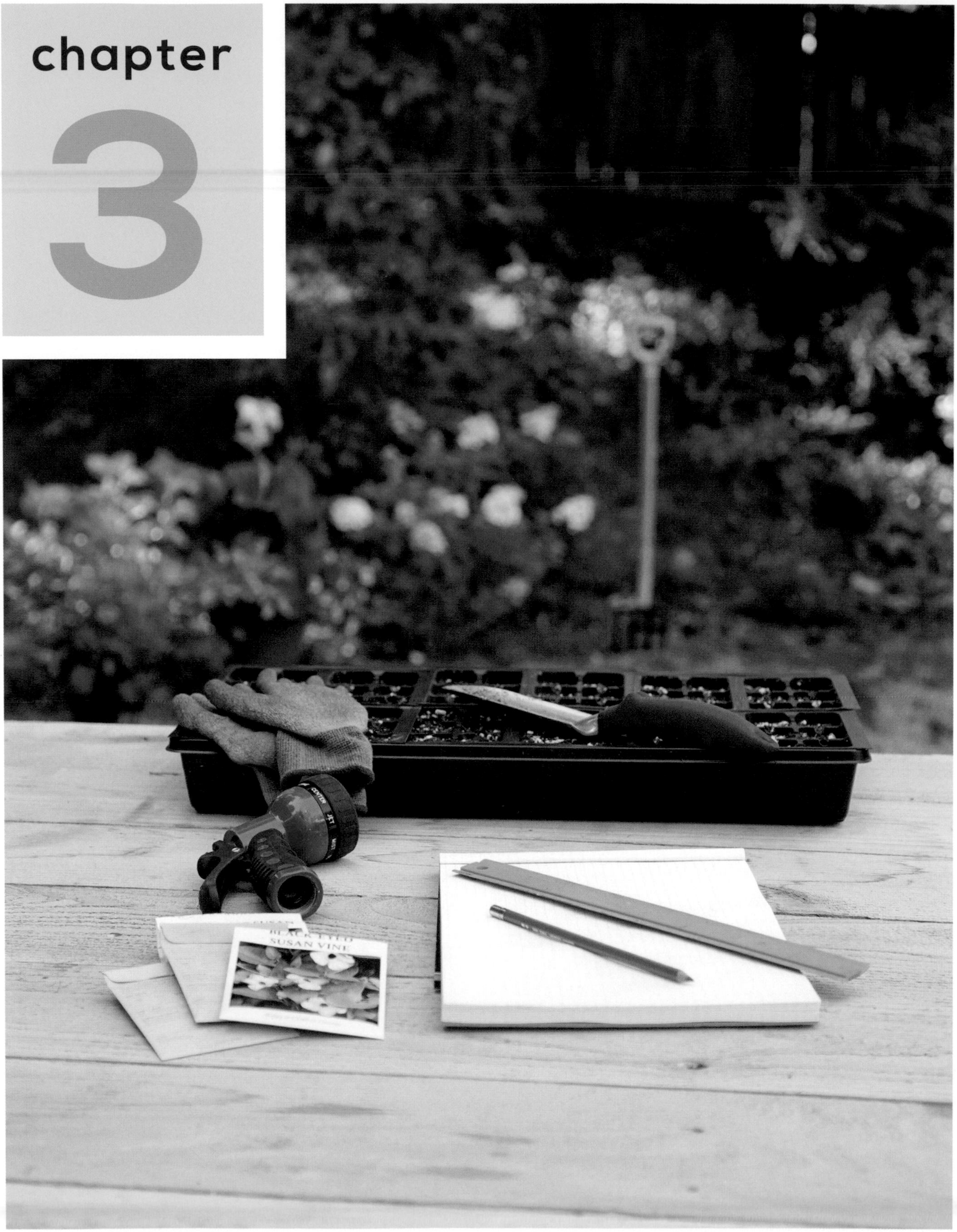

Getting Prepared for Your Garden:
taking inventory, tools, and more

As with any new task or project, it is essential to first prepare and form a game plan. Gardening is no different. However, new gardeners often struggle in the beginning of this process because everything seems so overwhelming, which leads to frustration and possibly giving up on their garden—but not you. Your garden preparation phase will begin with a basic activity that usually gets overlooked. You will get to know your own garden space.

By becoming familiar with the characteristics of your garden, including its layout and features, you can avoid painful garden care headaches later. For example, if you were to visualize your garden or verbally describe it to someone, how would you explain its overall appearance or shape? Could you describe what features are present? Are there tall trees nearby? You will soon know these answers.

In addition to the physical appearance of your garden, what types of plants and flowers do you hope to add, and what are their needs? Soon you'll discover if you have more shade or sun in your growing space and at what time of day the sun crosses your garden. Each garden is unique, and after a simple walk around your yard or balcony, you will be pleasantly surprised by how much you can learn in just a short amount of time. That is why before you are ready to grow or tend to your new plants (it is coming up soon, we promise!), there are a few important details you need to gather first.

Toward the end of the chapter, you will prepare for all of your upcoming garden care tasks by learning about the most important hand tools necessary for success. Having the right tool for the right job is essential to good garden care. From a garden trowel to pruning loppers to a tool called a hula hoe (what the heck is a hula hoe?), you will learn which tools you need to have in your toolbox, for which specific task each tool is used, and what each tool looks like. By the end of this chapter, you will be primed and ready to grow new plants and flowers.

taking an inventory of your garden

In the business world, a basic inventory consists of taking a count, or making a list, of certain goods or products to increase efficiency in some way. Wait! Before we bore you to tears with this definition, think of it this way: How would you feel if you just finished planting beautiful, *sun-loving* plants and flowers only to discover they will be located in full shade all summer due to an overhead deciduous tree that recently leafed out? Probably crushed, right? Luckily, this can all be avoided from the start with a bit of additional planning.

Going forward, you need to think about how all the pieces of your current garden space fit together, similar to the puzzle you started last chapter. Where is the sunlight located, and for how long does it reach your garden spot? How close is your garden's access to water? These are additional pieces of your garden puzzle that need to fit together perfectly to help your plants survive and thrive. Taking an inventory will require you to actually walk around your garden space to find the answers, most likely multiple times. Call it a garden "quest" or a "scavenger hunt," and at the end, you will uncover specific details about your unique garden *in advance* of planting or caring for it. It might sound tedious, but you will thank yourself later.

Taking inventory of this undeveloped garden bed is a great place to start your planning.

Create your garden goals prior to planting anything.

Here is what could happen if you avoid taking a garden inventory:

• Your plants might die because you could accidentally plant them in the wrong place and they wouldn't receive the level of sunlight they need to survive.

• Your plants might die because they are growing in the wrong soil. (Are you sensing a theme yet?)

• Your plants might not produce flowers because they are too stressed out due to too much water or not enough.

No one wants any of these scenarios to come true. A basic garden inventory should consist of locating your current plants in relation to each other, finding your available water sources, determining the types of soil you have in your garden, and so much more. For example, let's say you want to add pollinator-friendly plants and flowers to attract more pollinators. In this case, many of these plants will need full sun and could grow quite large. You would want to know how much sunlight and as growing space are available, for the new plants. If you want to create a container garden, then you need to know how close your water sources are located in addition to many other things related to plant care.

Time to begin your garden inventory! First, gather a writing utensil, lined paper or graph paper, a ruler, and a hard surface to write on as you walk around your garden. Sometimes it's helpful to draw a sketch of your garden space before finding your answers as recommended in the previous chapter. Your sketch can be as simple or as detailed as you want. There will not be any awards given for best artist. The more detailed you can make your sketch, the better, especially if you are a visual-minded, detail-oriented planner.

SETTING YOUR GARDEN GOALS

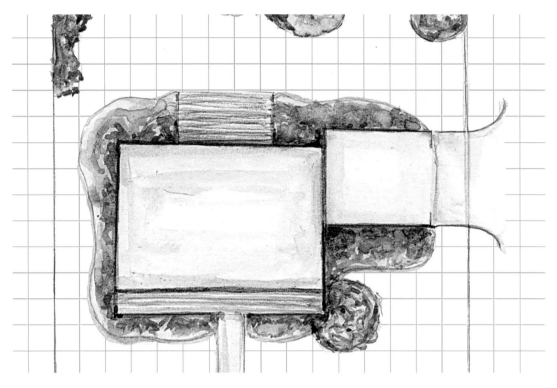

Drawing a simple sketch on graph paper is a great way to begin your garden inventory. This will serve as a template you can use for garden design, planning, and layout.

Have you ever thought about why you want to grow plants or flowers, or why you want to learn how to tend to them? Setting a garden goal is a crucial step in getting prepared for your garden. There are so many amazing reasons to get outside and grow new plants. It really is a personal decision. A lot of people garden for their health or because they wish to simply begin a new hobby. Other gardeners enjoy tending to flowers for the overall challenge of it or to attract more pollinators. Knowing your gardening "why" in advance can lead to better success and commitment. Just like any new adventure or hobby, taking the time to jot down (or at least think about) your goals before beginning can help you focus. Goal setting can also help you learn from your mistakes as you continue gardening in the future. Whatever your reasons for learning how to become a better gardener, good for you for embarking on this new adventure!

Next, depending on your overall goals for your garden space, you can break up your garden into sections so it will be easier to inventory. This might mean dividing your garden into "front" and "back" yards or "right" and "left" sides of your garden—whatever makes sense to your unique space.

Next, you will need to start locating specific characteristics of your garden. Follow each step below, in order, as you walk around your garden taking inventory. These steps could take anywhere from a few minutes to a few days to complete, depending on how detailed and thorough you want to be. Record your answers on your graph paper sketch or on lined paper if you so choose. Ready to begin your garden "scavenger hunt"?

1. CURRENT PLANTS

First, walk around your intended garden space, however large or small it may be, and take note of the types of plants you already have. Do you have mostly shrubs, perennials, annuals, or a mix of all three? How closely are they planted? How mature are they? It is okay if you have no idea. Just make your best guess and make notes on your sketch.

This is important to know because the space available for each plant to grow to its mature size needs to be available. You may find that you need to make space for new plants by removing older or larger plants that could crowd them out, change your garden location, or choose different plants.

2. AVAILABLE WATER SOURCES

Next, walk around your garden and locate all of your hose spigots, rain barrels, or any other sources of water you may have. How many water sources do you have? Where are they located? Mark these on your sketch for future reference.

This is important to know because as you are setting up your new garden, or adding to an existing garden, you need to take notice of how far away your water is from the garden. This is crucial.

More importantly, you need to plan how you will bring water to your new plants. If the water sources are too far from your garden and you feel like that may cause problems down the road, you may need to consider moving your garden somewhere closer to the existing water or adding more water pipe if you're into that kind of thing.

3. EXISTING SOIL TEXTURE

Soil texture includes all the sand, silt, or clay particles that mix together to make up your soil. This is important to know for many reasons but mainly because you would not want to add plants to the wrong type of soil, obviously. Don't worry if you have no idea

how much clay may or may not be in your soil or the combination of sand to silt. Later in this chapter, you will learn how to test your garden's soil texture using one of two methods. For now, just know that this part of your garden inventory will be continued later.

4. GARDEN CARDINAL DIRECTION

The sun shines on us at an angle at all times; it never shines directly overhead. This angle changes throughout the seasons because the Earth is tilted, but let's not get into planetary science right now. You need to understand how the sun's angle affects *your* garden so you know how much sunlight you have available. First, draw a compass on your graph paper to indicate the cardinal directions as related to your garden. To find your cardinal directions, use your phone's compass or a real compass to find north, south, east, and west.

Next, beginning early in the morning, track in what direction the sun is shining on your garden. What about afternoon sun or evening?

This is crucial to know because:

- In general, if your garden faces north, this area will get the least amount of sun.

- If your garden faces south, this area will get the highest amount of sun.

- If your garden faces east, this area will get the highest amount of sun in the morning.

- If your garden faces west, this area will get the highest amount of sun in the afternoon.

5. SUNLIGHT DURATION

How long does the sun track, or move across, your garden on a typical spring or summer day? Knowing this information will give you a good idea of when sunlight is available for your plants and where they will be best suited for their growing needs (i.e., full sun, partial sun, or full shade). Plants that need full sun will require six or more hours of daily sunlight to thrive. On the other hand, plants that need partial sun will only require three to four hours of sunlight. Full-shade plants require little to no direct sun. As you can see, that is quite a difference in available light levels. Begin by noticing what time sunlight first shines on your property, how long the sunlight is available throughout the day, and when it is no longer shining on your garden. You might consider describing its motion throughout one whole day or possibly multiple days, as needed. Furthermore, without getting too technical, the angle of the sun and, therefore, the sunlight duration *and* direction will change throughout the seasons due to the Earth's tilt, so keep that in mind, too.

Now, put together the duration of sunlight with your cardinal directions around your garden. In the southwest-, southeast-, northwest-, and northeast-facing directions of your garden, how many hours of light do they receive? Are there any tall trees, fences, or buildings that shade parts of these areas? This is what you must try to track and mark down in your inventory to help know which plants will do the best in those areas.

6. GARDEN OBSTRUCTIONS

Walk around your garden and notice if there are any buildings, tall trees, hedges, or other obstructions surrounding your garden. These tall features could greatly affect how much direct sunlight, and possibly rainwater, could reach your intended garden space. Plus, they might cause shade where you don't want shade. You marked some of this down in the previous section, but here make notes on your garden sketch where these obstructions actually are, if you haven't already.

7. GARDEN FEATURES

What features or points of interest are located in your garden, such as paths, fire pits, walkways, and the like? Knowing where all your walkways, pathways, patios, decks, buildings, and entrances are located will help you predict where you can expect foot traffic and help you avoid planting anything in these areas that could unintentionally get trampled on later. Make note of them on your sketch to reference later.

8. UTILITY HAZARDS

The final step in your scavenger hunt is to locate potential utility lines, pipes, or other important features buried underground. Take another walk around your property and locate any of these household utilities and where they are located in relation to your garden space. This is important to know for so many reasons but mainly for safety and also to ensure you don't build on top of, damage, or otherwise disturb those utilities on your property. This crucial step could help you eliminate any hazardous situation in the future.

Congratulations on finishing your garden inventory! You now have a lot of new information to use for all of your future garden planning. This garden knowledge will help you begin to think about what your new garden will look like, the amount of sunlight that is available, how you will move through your garden, and many other important considerations. But wait, there's even more (there's always more to know, right?). Another characteristic of your garden to know is to understand soil and determine its texture so your current and future plants will thrive better under your care.

"CALL BEFORE YOU DIG"

Calling before you dig in any areas surrounding your home can save you time, money, and lots of headaches. When planning small improvements around your home related to gardening, you wouldn't want to accidentally damage any utilities that could impact you or your neighbors, especially if these utilities are related to electrical, gas, water, sewer, telecommunications, or anything else. By calling first, you can make sure you are mindful of possible city, county, state/province, or federal laws affecting your property. Your bank account and insurance agent will be very thankful.

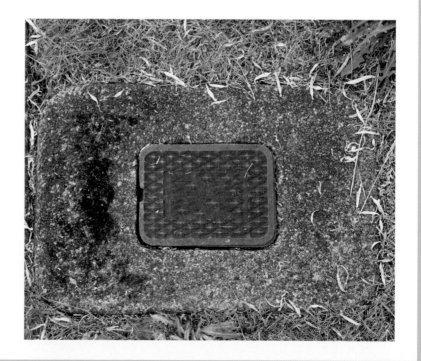

your soil texture and how to find it

Once you've jotted down this important information about your garden space, it's time to build on your knowledge of soil texture from the previous chapter. As you now know, soil is made up of three main textures (sand, silt, and clay). Soil also has different levels of organic matter mixed with it which have a direct impact on the health of your plants. If you remember, the larger the particles are in your soil (like sand), the more open spaces there will be around each particle. And the opposite is true for the smaller soil particles (like clay)—the less space or smaller areas there will be around each particle.

Therefore, before you buy any new plants or flowers, it helps to understand what texture soil you have. That way, you can match new plants and their soil needs to see if it is a good fit with your current garden soil. Otherwise, you will need to amend your soil or build new soil using various materials and methods (which you will learn about in Chapter 5).

Soil is made up of various particles, including sand, silt, and clay.

WHY IT IS IMPORTANT TO HAVE THE RIGHT KIND OF SOIL FOR YOUR PLANTS

Understanding the breakdown of your garden's soil, even the surface stuff (pun intended), will help you choose the right plants for your garden and tend to their needs. In addition to keeping the plant alive, using the correct soil has many other benefits, including:

• Proper nutrition for the plant

• Proper amount of water retention so that the plant doesn't drown in water, or lack water, due to incorrect soil texture

• Good air movement in the soil so plant roots can breathe

• Lower susceptibility to diseases or insects

• Good and secure anchor in its physical location so it does not uproot, topple over, and blow away unintentionally.

After making your garden soil into a ball, roll it between your hands to make a thin ribbon.

With the ribbon between your thumb and index finger, start pushing your thumb forward repeatedly to move the soil away from you. The longer the ribbon becomes, the more clay you have in your soil. The sooner the ribbon falls from your hand or disintegrates, the more sand you have in your soil.

how to test your soil's texture

There are many different ways to test your soil to determine what proportion of clay, sand, or silt you may have. Once you understand the breakdown of your soil, you can then modify it as needed by adding materials that can help change or enhance your current soil. But first, let's figure out what kind of soil you have using either the "Thumb-Ribbon" test or through water and dish soap.

The first easy way to determine your soil's texture is the "Thumb-Ribbon" test. You will need a hand trowel or small shovel, a rake, and a small cup of water. First, begin by digging a small hole (6 to 12 inches [15.2 to 30.5 cm]) in the soil. Loosen the soil with your trowel and grab a handful of it. Add water to the soil while still holding it in your hand and roll it into a ball. Next, roll the ball of soil into a long, cylinder shape or ribbon. If it starts to fall apart at this point, then you know you have a mostly sandy soil. If it keeps its rolled shape, then position it in your hand so you can place your thumb at the top of it and push your thumb forward over it, slowly making the soil move away from your thumb and hand. That's the start of your ribbon. If the soil keeps its form or shape, continue to do this until it falls and breaks apart.

The general idea here is that the longer your thumb-ribbon is, the more clay particles you have in your soil. The shorter the ribbon or the sooner it falls or breaks apart, then the more sand or pebbles you have in your soil.

This can be kind of messy, but it's a fun way to see and feel the soil texture you have in your garden. Additionally, this will give you a much better idea of how your soil drains along with how your plants will interact and grow in your garden. To watch a demonstration of the thumb-ribbon test, visit Chapter 3 of our Bonus Companion Guide at spokengarden.com/ftgbonusguide.

Another way to ascertain your soil texture is to purchase a soil testing kit. There are various soil texture testing kits to choose from, ranging from simple to more complicated. Most kits provide directions on how to use their product and how to read the results. These kits usually take 12 to 24 hours to produce results and can be inexpensive. Some kits are super easy to use with common household supplies, like water, dish soap, and a glass container with a lid. Using these supplies, you can add your soil to the glass container, add a small amount of dish soap on top of your soil, and then add water. Finally, secure the lid on the container. Shake well for about a minute and let sit for 12 hours or more to get your results.

A third option is to call a professional to come to your home and test your soil. Or they can send you a container and instructions to take a sample of your soil and send it back to them for analysis. At varying levels of cost, depending on the level of soil analysis you wish to discover, a professional might be able to give you a much more accurate measure of your soil texture. If you prefer this, you can contact your local garden agency or conservation district or research online to find out how to get started.

In general, if you have more sand in your soil, then you will need to water more frequently if you have any plants that grow better with regular watering. If you have more clay in your soil, then you can keep a modest regular watering schedule of maybe once or twice a week for any plants that need regular watering.

Once you have determined your garden's soil texture, you will gain a greater insight into your garden's overall health, possible water drainage issues, or any future problems that could arise due to your soil. Plus, shopping for new plants and flowers just got a whole lot easier.

Find your soil texture by using your garden soil, water, dish soap, and a clear glass container.

tools of the trade

A final important step in preparing for successful garden care is becoming familiar with the tools of the trade. These are the rock stars of your garden—your go-to collection of hand tools for digging, weeding, pruning, mulching, fertilizing, and so much more. Sure, your hands can be used for some of these tasks, but for best results you need the proper tools. A good pair of garden gloves wouldn't hurt either.

You might wonder which specific tool you would need for a particular garden task, and that is a fair question. There are so many tools and options from which to choose. However, several of these tools have multiple uses. For example, a fan rake can be used for both raking leaves and for pushing debris similar to a broom. Over time, you will develop your own uses for various garden tools to fit your needs.

Hand Trowel

Fan Rake

hand trowel Best for digging small planting holes, hand weeding, bulb planting, and other minor tasks

fan rake Best for collecting smaller, lighter debris or moving materials including leaves, small gravel, or mulch; also used for leaf collection over hard surfaces

Round Shovel

Bow Rake

Hula

Square Shovel

round shovel Best for digging new planting holes or transplanting plants and flowers; also for moving or mixing soil material

bow rake Best for moving heavier materials, like larger mulch and gravel; also great for collecting larger debris

square shovel Best for edging and creating straight lines around beds

hula (stirrup hoe) Best for weeding shallow-rooted weeds in garden beds and for maintaining or creating bed edges

Garden Hoe

Spading (Garden) Fork

Pruning Handsaw

garden hoe Best for weeding deep-rooted weeds and for bed preparation for planting

spading (garden) fork Best for loosening soil before weeding and breaking up hard soil around the garden

pruning handsaw Best for cutting and removing larger branches when loppers won't work

pitchfork Best for moving materials like mulch, leaves, compost, and more around your garden

Pitchfork

Wheelbarrow

Small Tarp

wheelbarrow Best for moving plants, mulch, soil, wood, gravel, debris, and other materials around your garden as needed

small tarp Best for collecting and moving plants or other materials around your garden

pruning shears Best for cutting and removing small branches, twigs, flowers, and roots for plant health, shaping, planting, or transplanting

loppers Best for cutting and removing larger branches from shrubs and trees; similar to pruning shears but for larger cuts

Pruning Shears

Loppers

time to plant!

Now that you are familiar with the characteristics of your garden, including its layout and features, you have a better sense of what features make up your garden, where water is located, and so much more. You are finally ready to graduate to planting and beginning to grow your plants and flowers. Are you excited? Get ready to learn how to plant seeds, seedlings, and more coming up next in Chapter 4.

Tools come in all shapes of sizes and can be used for many things.

SAVE YOUR HANDS AND THE ENVIRONMENT WITH BAMBOO GLOVES OR TOOLS

Bamboo is a renewable, sustainable resource. This plant, one of the fastest growing on our planet, is extremely versatile for use in different products, including garden and work gloves, tools, tool handles, plant stakes, garden edging, and even home flooring. Next time you are looking for new tools or gloves, consider a product made from bamboo.

KEY TAKEAWAYS FROM THIS CHAPTER:

- Taking an inventory of your garden is one of the most important steps before designing or planting.

- Testing your garden soil determines what combination of soil texture you have.

- Having the right tool for the right job will make taking care of your garden so much easier.

DIG DEEPER

It's important to make sure you are using your garden hand tools correctly. We'll show you a tutorial about how to use hand tools in your garden and also how to find your garden's soil texture by demonstrating the thumb-ribbon test. This will be in Chapter 3 of the Bonus Companion Guide. Check it out at spokengarden.com/ftgbonusguide.

Planting Your Garden:
steps, tips, and common mistakes

Properly planting seeds, seedlings, plants, and bulbs can make a huge difference between whether your plants thrive or die in their new home. Planting not only influences how to physically place them in a specific location but is one of the key measures of their survival. In this chapter you will not only learn how to plant a seed, seedling, immature plant, or bulb, you'll also learn planting mistakes to avoid and the advantages of planting each size, or maturity level, of plant in your garden. This will help you build healthy plants from the beginning and quicken each plant's establishment period in your garden, especially if you intend to plant a seedling or plant of immature size. Prepare to have your mind blown. You are about to create, and then grow, a whole new plant. It is time to dig in, literally.

a few considerations before you plant anything

Soon you will learn how to grow plants at different stages of their life, or maturity levels. Whether you want to grow a plant from seed, seedling, semi-mature plant, or bulb (your choice, by the way), let's clear up a few things before we get started so you are prepped and ready to grow plants.

- Plants have basic needs. All of the plant stages below have the same basic needs to grow and flower, including light, soil, water, and the right temperature. They just require different amounts of these basic needs.

- The sequence of planting instructions below are appropriate whether you plan to plant directly in the ground or straight into a container. The choice of planting location is yours; the planting instructions are not. Follow the steps below for the greatest chance for the plant's survival as they are moved into their new homes.

- Even with your best intentions, some plants will throw a tantrum as they react to their new home. If you've ever moved to a new home, you may already know what this means. Plants have an establishment period during which time they must acclimate. In more extreme cases, some plants even experience "transplant shock." You see, plants experience shock due to drastic life changes just like we do. After moving into their new home (whether ground or container), plants may suffer through this period of distress and react accordingly. Some plants show very little physical evidence of going through this shock. They may continue to grow, once planted, but minimally at first. This could last up to a year. Other plants might display harsher signs of transplant shock by their leaves curling or wilting, turning yellow, or parts of the plant completely dying. This is life cycle specific, so be prepared.

- Bulbs are unique. Compared to seeds or seedlings, they have a different set of rules. While they are still a plant, they are a specific *type* of plant; a specialized underground root or stem base. They store their energy and nutrients inside their little bodies, then grow from this stored energy each year. This is why bulbs are set apart from the other forms of planting because they have specific planting and handling requirements of their own.

- You will need a few tools. In general, you'll need to gather the following tools: gloves, a rake (to clear any debris or mulch from a planting area), a hand trowel (for digging trenches and holes), possibly a round shovel (for digging larger plant holes or larger planting areas), and maybe pruning shears (to cut and separate tougher plant roots of the semi-mature plants). Also, you should have a hose or watering can available to water your new plants immediately after planting.

This little seed has the potential to grow into a plant 6 or 7 feet (1.8 or 2.1 m) tall with a dinner plate–sized flower in less than 5 months.

growing by seed

DEFINITION

Before you have a beautiful plant to admire, you have a seed. A seed is a flowering plant's offspring, capable of developing into a whole new plant.

ADVANTAGE OF SEEDS

The advantages of growing a plant by seed is the personal care you can take in that plant's development by watching it grow from its very beginning. Also, this is an inexpensive way to grow plants. The downside to growing from seed is that it takes longer to grow a big enough plant to then plant out into your garden, either in the ground or in a container. This is a great way for you to practice your plant care skills to hone in on when to water, how much light or dark each seed needs to germinate and to grow, and when to then transplant it to a larger container or into your garden bed.

There is a great variety in plant seed size.

PREPARATION BEFORE PLANTING

To be prepared to plant your seeds, you will need some supplies. Mainly you will need some seed starting soil for both indoor and outdoor planting, of which there are many different brands to choose from. Make sure it is specifically designed for starting seeds and has good drainage. You will also need to supply most seeds with a constant warm temperature of 55°F (13°C) or higher while keeping the soil moist, especially around the seed, for them to have the highest chance to germinate.

When planting seeds, you will need to make sure that the soil in which you sow your seeds drains well. Also, either have seed starting soil or some finer soil, like vermiculite, to place over the seeds once sown so they have either a light or deeper covering of soil that can keep moisture close to the seeds to enhance and quicken germination. Be sure to follow the seed packet instructions on how much space to have between each seed and how deeply to plant them. Also, be sure to pre-water the seed starting soil before planting seeds so the soil is already wet and can be in direct contact with each seed when planted. Using mist, spray to wet the seeds and soil over the seeds after planting to ensure that the seeds and soil are not displaced.

top left First, make a trench to place the seeds in. **top right** Carefully place the seeds in the trench. **bottom right** Then cover the seeds lightly by filling back in the trench.

how to plant seeds

Your first step is to prep your soil in which you are planting your seeds. This means to loosen up and break apart any soil chunks either in your garden bed (if sowing directly) or in the seed starting soil. Make sure to level and smooth out the soil and then water it before planting. If you need to make a row in your garden or create small holes in the seed starting soil, do this now. Then plant your seeds according to their prescribed planting depth and soil covering needs. Lightly tamp down that soil over the seeds and then lightly water with fine mist or give a light watering with a nozzle. Now you will need to wait until your seeds germinate and break through the soil to then start growing up. This can take anywhere from 5 to 21 days or more before you visibly see any plants growing up out of the soil.

If you are planting seeds outside directly in your garden, be sure to keep an eye on the water and give your seeds any protection they may need from cooler temperatures, hard rain, or any other extreme weather that they will not like. And keep an eye out for those first primordial and then first true set of leaves.

PLANTING STEPS

If sowing your seeds directly out in your garden beds:

1. Clear the area of any mulch or other debris.

2. Prep your soil by fluffing it up with a hand trowel or rake.

3. Dig your hole or make your trench.

4. Leave the mulch clear of this area.

5. Sow (place) your seeds at the correct planting depth by placing them in either your garden bed or in seed starting soil.

6. Cover with fine soil or vermiculite to the appropriate depth.

7. Water again lightly with mist spray or very gently on a regular basis from this point forward regularly.

If you are planting in seed starting soil inside:

1. Prep by filling trays and cells with soil.

2. Water the soil before sowing seeds.

3. Wet the soil down.

4. Sow (place) your seeds at the correct planting depth by placing them in seed starting soil.

5. Cover with fine soil or vermiculite to the appropriate depth.

6. Water again lightly with mist spray or very gently on a regular basis from this point forward.

AVOID THESE PLANTING MISTAKES

Now that you have read how to generally plant seeds, here are a few mistakes to watch for and how to avoid them. First, if you plant seeds too deep or too shallow, there is a very good possibility that they won't germinate. In addition, if you are direct sowing outside in your garden, birds and other wildlife can more easily find and eat your seeds, too, so keep this in mind when planting seeds to sow them at the correct depth. Next, if you give your seeds too much water, they might not germinate and could rot in the soil. If you give seeds too little water, they also might not germinate. But once germinated and they don't get enough water, they can wilt and die fairly quickly. So, keep up on watering and know when to water and not to water. Consistently moist soil is your best bet, but don't drown them.

PLANTING HACK

The smaller the seed, the closer to the surface you should plant it. Conversely, the larger the seed, the deeper you should plant it (but always follow the directions on the seed packet if it is available).

CARE AFTER PLANTING

After planting your seeds, your job now is to monitor their water needs. The soil needs to remain wet and it needs to be kept generally at that constant temperature of 55°F (13°C) or higher, depending on that specific plant (again, refer to the seed packet). Once your seeds have germinated, continue to monitor them for water and begin to watch their growth and check for any insects or yellowing of their leaves. If any of this happens, isolate those plants to protect other plants, then find the correct treatment.

There are many plants and flowers you can start by seed: sunflowers, alyssum, zinnia, cosmos, aster, China aster, black-eyed Susan, coneflower, and many more.

grow by seedling

DEFINITION

A seedling is a newly germinated seed with at least one or two pairs of true leaves, or more.

ADVANTAGES OF SEEDLINGS

Zinnia flower seedlings emerging from the soil after germinating.

The advantage of buying and planting a seedling in your garden is that you do not have to go through the whole germination process. You can cheat a bit. And, it will be closer to flowering (hopefully). Seedlings found at nurseries will be both annual and perennial plants. If the threat of frost has passed in the spring season, these small plants are now tough enough to be planted in your garden. It will then be safe for them to continue to grow and thrive compared to the directly sowed seeds.

PREPARATION BEFORE PLANTING

Let's practice what you learned in Chapter 2 about plant spacing. First, you need to plan where you want your seedling to live in your garden and if there will be enough space for it to grow to its full mature size. Next, the soil you plant your seedling into needs to be moderate to well draining, and you should add and mix any compost or other soil amendments to the soil before planting begins.

Carefully remove the seedling from the seed tray cell without damaging the plant stem or leaves.

Make sure to break up and spread the seedling roots before planting in new soil.

Before planting seedlings, clear away any debris or mulch from your planting area to expose the surface of your garden soil. Pre-dig your planting hole. In general, you won't need to dig a large hole. The old trick is, dig your hole twice as wide as the root ball of the seedling. The hole should only be as deep as the root ball, no deeper. Finally, make sure to water your planting hole at this point so your new plant will have water readily available at planting.

PLANTING HACK

The seedling's planting depth in your garden bed needs to match its planting depth that it came from in its previous container.

PLANTING STEPS FOR SEEDLINGS

1. Clear the area of any mulch or other debris.

2. Prep your soil by fluffing it up.

3. Add compost or other soil amendment, and then fully mix it together with the old soil.

4. Dig your hole twice as wide as the seedling's root ball.

5. Wet the soil down.

6. Carefully loosen the seedling's roots. Sometimes plants will have circling roots in their container. Often you will need to untangle and straighten them out from being in the shape of the container before planting. Then gently place your seedling in the hole.

7. Lightly cover the seedling's roots with soil. Continue to cover until the hole is filled in and then lightly tap the soil down.

8. Re-spread the area with mulch, being careful not to place mulch up against your new plant's stem.

9. Water again lightly.

CARE AFTER PLANTING

Once your seedling has been planted in your garden, you will need to keep up a regular watering schedule according to that plant's needs, and some plants will have different watering needs from others, so be sure to plant plants together that have the same watering needs, like you read in Chapter 2.

PLANTING MISTAKES TO AVOID

When planting seedlings, you want to avoid planting the small plant either too high or too low as compared to the surrounding soil of your garden or container. An easy way to make sure you plant a seedling at the right depth in soil is to notice the seedling's current soil depth before planting. If it is healthy and thriving at that soil depth, it should be at the same depth after you've transplanted it to its new home. Keep that soil planting depth the same and you will avoid the seedling rotting, wilting, drooping, or having other growth problems in your garden.

grow by semi-mature plant

DEFINITION

A semi-mature plant is one that is larger than a seedling. In general, it is any plant that is in a pot larger than 4 inches (10 cm) and has flower buds growing or ready to open. Some semi-mature plants may also be in full flower.

A semi-mature daphne shrub ready to be planted in your garden.

Dig a hole in your container to the proper planting depth.

Before planting, break up the plant's roots.

As you place the plant roots in the hole, splay out its roots from the center of the plant and hole.

Backfill your plant hole with the soil you removed and lightly tamp the soil down before watering.

ADVANTAGES OF PLANTING A SEMI-MATURE PLANT

The advantage of planting this mature stage is that you get almost instant color and texture and a more fully formed plant that can really start to fill in a planting space. Establishing this size of plant is often easier.

AVOID THESE PLANTING MISTAKES

A very common mistake new gardeners make when planting this size plant is planting it too low or too high in its new planting hole. If planted too low, it can develop stem and root rots that can eventually kill the plant. If planted too high, plant roots are usually exposed above the ground; this can dry those roots out and leave them exposed to weather extremes. The plant can not only dry out fast; it can also have leaf die-back along with less flowering or overall growth. To avoid either of these mistakes, make sure to place your plants at the same depth in your garden as they were in their pots before you planted them. Larger trees and shrubs, in pot sizes of 2 gallons (7.6 L) or bigger, will also flare out at the base of their stem right before it goes into the soil. Where this flare is can be a good indication of where the soil level for planting should be. The flare should sit just above the soil's surface.

Here is a good example of planting too high, showing how the upper plant roots are exposed.

PLANTING STEPS FOR SEMI-MATURE PLANTS

1. Clear the area of any mulch or other debris.

2. Prep your soil by fluffing it up and breaking up soil chunks.

3. Add compost, sand, and the like and then fully mix it together with the old soil—if soil amending is needed.

4. Dig your hole. Bonus tip: Make a small mound in the bottom center of the hole.

5. Wet the soil down.

6. Gently place your plant in the hole (on top of the mound), making sure to break up the roots, especially if they were circling around inside the pot.

7. Refill the hole with soil until the hole is filled in. Then lightly tap the soil down.

8. Create a berm (or a dike) around the entire perimeter of the planting hole to channel irrigation water.

9. Re-spread the area with mulch, being careful not to place mulch up against your new plant's stem.

10. Water again lightly.

CARE AFTER PLANTING

Once your plant is placed in your garden, now is when you will need to make sure it is getting regular scheduled watering, along with any removal of dead or fallen flowers, leaves, or other debris. Keep your garden tidy and clean to lessen insect and disease damage. Some plants may require staking or another support for their flower stems to keep them growing upright.

PLANTING HACK

Dig your planting hole twice as wide as the root mass to make it easier for the roots to grow and spread out over time.

grow by bulb

DEFINITION

A bulb is a specialized, underground root or stem-like structure that stores energy and nutrients from which plants can grow.

One of the most popular fall-planted, spring-flowering bulbs is a daffodil.

A LITTLE ABOUT BULBS

Bulb plants are used mainly in gardens for their bright color or interesting foliage, especially in late winter to early spring but also late spring and through summer. They are enjoyed for their seasonal accents and ease of care. Once planted, as long as they're hardy in your climate, bulbs will emerge at the right time of year on their own. They usually flower for a few weeks.

Bulbs are divided into two groups: spring-flowering and summer-flowering. The quirky part of bulbs is this: Spring-flowering bulbs need to be planted the prior fall, about 6 to 8 weeks before the first frost arrives. Summer-flowering bulbs need to go in the ground in the spring, usually after the threat of frost has passed and your garden soil is at or above 50°F (10°C). Most of the time, once either of the spring- or summer-flowering bulbs is established in your garden, it will continue to come back year after year as long as the varieties you choose are hardy in your climate.

Bulbs are an entire subset of gardening. Enjoyed for their uniqueness and intricate in their different storage structures (there are five different kinds of bulbs), seasonal flowering, flower shapes, breeding, and a whole lot more, the proper handling and placement of bulbs can make the difference between bulbs that bloom and those that do not.

ADVANTAGES

A few advantages to growing bulbs are their unique ability to be easily handled and mass planted in containers or along garden edges or other areas for early flowering in the spring when most plants in your garden are still dormant. Flower forms and colors are also unique, for either spring- or summer-flowering bulbs, so having them in your garden can help you stand apart from your neighbors. This is especially true when planting bulbs in groupings, where you should always use odd numbered plantings of three, five, seven, nine, and beyond. This can give your garden an extra edge in vibrancy and fullness.

Can you tell which is the daffodil bulb and which is the tulip bulb?

AVOID THESE PLANTING MISTAKES

One planting mistake for bulbs is planting each bulb too shallow or too deep. If you plant a bulb too shallow, it might still emerge from the soil, but it will fall over and not be anchored well. It also may freeze out during the winter. If a bulb is planted too deeply, you probably will never see it again because it lacked the proper temperature and/or moisture to signal its growth cycle. To avoid planting either too shallow or too deep, follow the general rule of planting each bulb to a depth equal to two to three times its height. This means that if a bulb is 3 inches (7.6 cm) tall, the proper planting depth is approximately 6 to 9 inches (15.2 to 22.9 cm). You can also read the specific planting instructions of the bulb packaging, if still available at the time of planting.

Another planting mistake is incorrect planting due to their proper orientation or placement. Some teardrop-shaped bulbs, like tulips or daffodils, are easier to orient when planting compared to bulbs that are shaped like potatoes or rocks or are skinny-topped and fat-bottomed shapes, like dahlias. Any bulb that is teardrop shaped can be oriented so that its pointy tip is facing up. If the bulb is more of a donut or round-flattened shape, there will be a slight indented surface on one of the flatter areas that needs to point up. Other bulbs shaped similar to a potato or a lumpy rock should be generally laid on their side in the planting hole. With these, you need to look for "eyes" or buds directly on them so you can orient those to face up.

Gladiolus bulbs need to be planted in the spring so they can flower in the summer.

CARE AFTER PLANTING

Bulb care after planting is easy and almost completely carefree. You really only have to make sure that once your bulbs have broken through the soil that they receive regular watering to keep them healthy until they are done flowering. Then, once the leaves have completely withered and turned brown down to the ground level, you can remove those dead leaves and you are done until next year when the flowers return on their own. Simple, right?

PLANTING HACK

Make sure to include any layers of mulch into the total depth of your planting hole. Otherwise, your bulb may be buried too deeply and it will be unable to find the surface or grow properly. If you want to plant your bulbs fast, you can use a mini-auger or bulb auger that attaches to your electric hand drill. Those planting holes will be dug quickly, and it's a lot of fun.

PLANTING STEPS FOR BULBS

1. Clear the area of any mulch or other debris.

2. Prep your soil if you need to improve the soil's nutrition and/or drainage by mixing in compost, sand, and the like.

3. Dig your hole according to which type of bulb you are planting (corm, tuber, etc.). You can dig a large hole and plant several bulbs per hole or dig an individual hole for each bulb.

4. Gently place your bulb in the hole in the proper orientation.

5. Lightly cover the bulb with soil. Continue to cover until the hole is filled in and then lightly tap the soil down.

6. Re-cover the area with mulch.

7. Water the area.

PLANTING IN A CONTAINER

A great advantage to planting in containers is that you can move them around to where you want, with "right plant, right place" in mind, of course. However, an important disadvantage to consider is that plants in containers will require more attention. This is due to the fact that because they are in their own mini ecosystem, they take more time, in general, to get the best care. Follow planting steps to place any plant in a container for that stage of plant.

Getting ready to plant in your container, make sure to have all your tools nearby.

ECO-FRIENDLY TIP:

USE CERTIFIED, ORGANICALLY SOURCED SUPPLIES FOR YOUR PLANT MATERIAL

When choosing your sources for seeds, plants, and bulbs, consider buying from companies that are certified organic growers and producers. These certified companies guarantee that their seeds and plants are never treated with synthetic chemicals or pesticides and are not grown using methods that contribute to pollution.

WHEN TO PLANT BULBS IN YOUR GARDEN

Fall-Planted Bulbs: daffodil, tulip, crocus, muscari, allium, hyacinth, iris

Spring-Planted Bulbs: liatris, crocosmia, dahlia, gladiolus, canna lily

you're a planting pro!

Planting seeds, seedlings, semi-mature plants, and even bulbs in your garden provides you with many different options to fit your garden's needs. Depending on which stage of plant maturity you choose to add to your garden, you can either enjoy slow and steady growth with minimal care or instant flower color. Bulbs offer seasonal interest, gifting you with spring or summer pops of color that other gardeners only wish they could have. Whatever and however you choose to plant, the options are endless. And with that, now you are ready to learn how to tend to all of your new plants and flowers.

KEY TAKEAWAYS FROM THIS CHAPTER

- There are minor differences between the planting steps for each plant stage.

- There are four general rules of planting for each stage: prep, plant, water, and check back.

- Bulbs are unique and can be sorted into fall-planted and spring-planted bulbs.

- The steps for each plant maturity stage can be used to plant in the ground or in a container.

DIG DEEPER

Watch us demonstrate how to orient and plant bulbs in Chapter 4 of the Bonus Companion Guide so you can better understand how to plant bulbs correctly in your garden. Check it out at spokengarden.com/ftgbonusguide.

Caring for Your Garden:
the what, when, and how

Plants are amazing in their ability to adapt and grow in so many different places. Progressing from their basic anatomy and function to how we can match them to our garden and plant them correctly, it's now time to learn how to care for them. Their survival is our goal. We want to keep encouraging our plants to grow and flower so we can see them mature in all their glory. But how do we care for them? What's involved, and where should you get started? This chapter is your ticket to Garden Care 101.

Between what you see above ground and what you can't see below ground, there is so much going on to keep your plants healthy. Your garden care tasks range from keeping your plants clean to shaping and pruning, mulching, pest control, and more. This chapter is packed with great information on each of these topics.

aboveground care

What you see above ground is only part of a whole plant. While it tends to be the part we focus on the most, the truth is that to really care for your plants, you have to focus on what's below the ground, too. But let's start with what we can see first. Your main goal in tending your plants is to keep their stress levels low by making sure they have enough water, minimal pests, plenty of nutrients, enough space to grow, no dead or diseased tissues, and a whole lot more. To do all this, you need to know how to properly mulch, prune, weed, control pests, and deadhead. You will learn about each of these important garden care tasks in the following pages.

Here is a withered bloom from an African daisy ready to be deadheaded.

DEADHEADING

Deadheading is when you physically remove any withered or dead flowers from that plant.

Deadhead your plants to keep them looking tidy and clean, to encourage more flowers to grow and bloom, and to keep your garden free of any dead tissue laying around that could encourage pests or diseases. It's important to know, however, that not all plants continue to produce flowers after they have been deadheaded. Some (peonies, tulips, and rhododendrons, for example) bloom once a year and then they're done, but many others produce a flush of new blooms when the spent flowers are removed.

To deadhead different plants in your garden, you can use a few hand tools. Any tool with a snipping or cutting mechanism or sharp blade works well for this, including hand shears, pruning snips, florist scissors, and different small knives. Some plants only

Use pruning shears to remove the old bloom by cutting just below the spent flower on the stem.

require you to pinch spent flowers off with your thumb and index finger, if you are comfortable doing that.

To deadhead, identify the old, dead, or withered bloom. As described in Chapter 1 of this book, flowers are attached to plants by a stem, whether short or long. This is where you need to remove the flower, along with the flowering stem (unless there are more buds that haven't opened yet, in which case you should wait a bit to deadhead). A clean cut or pinch is preferred, as opposed to tearing, because your plant will be able to heal faster from a clean separation. Once the flower and flower stem are removed, place them on a tarp or in a bucket. Continue to deadhead the rest of your garden, collecting all the old flowers and disposing of them on the compost pile. Walk around your garden on a weekly basis and deadhead as necessary.

MULCHING

Mulching is the placing and spreading of any material over your garden soil around your plants to benefit and improve your garden both above and below the ground. Most mulches also improve the appearance of your garden by offering specific characteristics of color and texture.

The act of mulching and using mulch in your garden is important for many different reasons. Overall, mulching helps maintain general plant health. Above ground, it is great for weed suppression and control, along with also creating different visual textures to either match or contrast your plant's leaf and flower color and shape. Below ground, mulch helps regulate plant roots and insulate them from temperature extremes. It minimizes soil compaction and soil erosion, increases soil moisture retention, and improves soil drainage. Mulches can also help improve soil structure and nutrition when they break down over time and filter down into your garden soil.

When you spread mulch in your garden, you will need a round and flat shovel, a pitchfork, wheelbarrow, and a bow rake.

First, fill up your wheelbarrow using a shovel or pitchfork.

Second, haul mulch to its intended location and dump it out into a pile.

Third, spread your mulch using your bow or hard rake.

Fourth, make sure your mulch is at least 2 inches (5 cm) away from the base of any plant tissue.

Mulching is one of the best ways to keep weed seeds from germinating. The reason for this is threefold: First, placing mulch over and around your garden soil and plants keeps sunlight, water, and soil temperatures low enough or blocked from reaching the right levels for a lot of weed seeds to germinate. Second, mulch in medium to larger sizes or textures makes it harder for weed seeds to germinate and get a good foothold in the material. Third, with a fresh layer of mulch spread, you can more easily see weeds germinating and pull them sooner.

Picking the right kind of naturally sourced mulch is important based on what your goal for mulching is. Most every gardener wants to add mulch to make their garden look better and more appealing, but also for many other reasons. There are many different kinds of mulch available, each with its own distinct appearance and benefits.

WHAT IS SHEET MULCHING?

Example of how to sheet mulch by using cardboard and newspaper.

Sheet mulching is a no-dig mulching technique used to establish a new garden bed with little soil disturbance to help build soils and squelch weeds. Use sheets of cardboard, newspaper, or another material that overlap to not let any sunlight through to the ground and then place a thick layer of mulch over the top of it.

TYPES OF NATURALLY SOURCED MULCHES AND THEIR BENEFITS

Arborist Mulch

Benefit: Long-lasting mulch great for preventing weeds from growing, plant root insulation, erosion control, soil building, and naturally adding nutrients for plants to use

Cedar Bark Mulch

Benefit: Mainly for aesthetic uses in a garden and good for weed suppression

Pine Needles

Benefit: Provides an interesting look to a garden, good for weed suppression, insulates soil or roots, and holds in moisture for plants

Rock Mulch (pebbles, drain, or river rock)

Benefit: Retains heat, controls erosion, and helps water drain fast

Lava Rock

Benefit: Provides unique visual texture with reddish-brown color, good for weed suppression and drainage, and controls erosion

Compost

Benefit: Great for increasing soil and plant nutrition and helping with soil texture building

Shredded Leaves

Benefit: Great eco-friendly way to reincorporate plant material back into your garden, along with increasing drainage, building soil structure, and suppressing weeds

Hazelnut Shells

Benefit: Great for weed suppression, water drainage, and providing your garden with a unique look

Straw (barley, hay)

Benefit: Great for soil erosion, weed suppression, and surface water drainage

Keep in mind that the larger the mulch piece size, the harder it is for weeds to germinate and get established in your garden. This is because the larger-sized mulches don't hold on to moisture or nutrients very well, letting both filter down through to the below soil. Mulches with smaller piece sizes like finer barks or compost, even if 2 to 4 inches (5 to 10 cm) thick, are much better for weeds to germinate in because they will drain slower and hold on to moisture and nutrients longer.

How to Mulch—Steps to Get It Done

1. Clean and clear away debris and weeds from the area of your garden you are going to add mulch to.

2. Re-level your garden soil by raking and smoothing it out.

3. Using your shovel, pitchfork, and wheelbarrow, start hauling and placing mulch in piles around your garden beds.

4. Use your bow rake to then spread the mulch around, leveling the mulch as you go and keeping it at 2 to 4 inches (5 to 10 cm) thick as consistently as you can around the garden.

To learn even more about spreading mulch around your plants, visit our Bonus Companion Guide to dig deeper into how close and how thick to spread your mulch. You can find it in Chapter 5 at spokengarden.com/ftgbonusguide.

MULCHING PRO TIPS

- Make sure to keep mulch a minimum of 2 inches (5 cm) away from any plant stems or bases so moisture can't collect around plant tissues to lead to issues such as rot, disease, or pests.

- If you are mulching during a drier time of year or if it's been unseasonably dry, be sure to water your plants and garden thoroughly before spreading mulch so you don't create an unintended drought situation later. Remember that mulch insulates and protects the soil below it, whether it is wet or dry. If it starts out dry, then it could stay that way longer if not watered first.

PEST CONTROL

Aphids infesting a
lupine plant's stems
and leaves.

A pest is any plant, insect, animal, fungus, bacterium, or virus that causes damage to your plants or impacts the garden's overall health. Any plant that is growing in your garden but wasn't planted by you (and is creating problems) is considered a pest, otherwise known as a weed. Some insects in your garden are considered pests because they negatively impact your garden plants. Other insects are beneficial because they prey on pest insects or pollinate your flowers. And there are certain animals that are garden pests because they eat or damage whole plants or parts of plants.

There are many different garden pests you might see in your garden. Pests can cause plant stress that leads to reduced growth, flowering, and perhaps other pest or disease infestations. The best thing to do is keep any pest damage to a minimum. With anything in nature, there is a balance that needs to be maintained. A few pests are normal and nothing to worry about, but when the damage they cause reaches a threshold you can't tolerate, it's time to take action.

When you decide to control or remove garden pests, you will need various tools to do this, depending on the pest and how you intend to control them. If you are weeding and removing any plants you did not intend to grow in your garden, then you will need a hand trowel, shovel, rake, and hula hoe to keep them under control. If you need to control a specific insect pest, like aphids, whiteflies, caterpillars, or slugs, then you will need to find a specific eco-friendly product or method to treat these pests.

Each pest is different, and you will need to look for signs and symptoms of that pest to know how best to solve the problem. Signs of damage are visible indications of a pest, but so is seeing the actual pest on or near your plants. Symptoms are how your plants are reacting to that damage or the physical effect the pest is having on your plant. For example, a plant might slow growth, change leaf shape or stem length, have holes in its leaves, or turn color. If you do use a purchased product, be sure to read the label and apply it only when you have identified the pest and that pest is included on that product's label. There are three eco-friendly ways to control pests in your garden: by DIY methods, products you can buy, and by the plants you have in your garden. You can see examples of these in "Eco-friendly Pest Control Methods" on page 57.

Before we talk about how to control pests in your garden, we need to tell you about the importance of prevention. Prevention is the best anti-pest strategy, and it begins by maintaining the best growing conditions for all your plants. This comes down to choosing the right plants for your garden, handling and planting correctly, watering, pruning, mulching, and maintaining overall garden cleanliness. If you can do all these things, then you can prevent most pests and garden problems. Stressed plants are a welcome mat for pests. Properly maintained plants are far less pest prone. If prevention isn't an option or you are past the preventing stage, then the following options will greatly help you.

Pest control can be broken down into five options. All are eco-friendly or can be naturally sourced, so not to worry. With any of these categories of pest control, the best one to choose depends on the pest itself and what is the best fit. Most gardeners will tell you that a combination of these categories is your best bet, but since you are new to gardening, try each one one at a time so you don't get overwhelmed. Once the first control category is started, you can then start a second one to add to it and see what results you get, adding other control categories as needed. Hopefully one or two of these categories will be all you need to take care of a particular pest problem. From here, you will find each control category name, what it is, and two examples of using it in your garden.

1. Physical Control
Physical control is the physical (by hand) removal of pests. This also works well for weed control and physically blocking certain animal pests from reaching your plants. Weeding your garden is the act of physically removing plants with a trowel or hula hoe. Blocking squirrels, rabbits, deer, and other animals with barriers or by moving plants out of the animal's reach are great controls.

2. Mechanical Control
Mechanical control is when you use a machine, like a rototiller, to control weeds. It also includes using sticky cards or tapes, pheromone traps or lures, or covering plants with floating row cover or tulle netting to control pests. This method is great for weed and insect control in your garden.

3. Environmental Control

Environmental control is great because you can change the garden environment to deter pests. Examples of this are changing your soil's drainage and increasing or decreasing sunlight levels, water availability, or other garden characteristics to make it harder for a pest to live or damage your plants. Environmental control works well with controlling weeds, insects, bacteria, fungi, viruses, and animals.

4. Biological Control

Biological control of pests is where you can use a pest's natural predators or diseases to eradicate or at least control their population. Examples of this are releasing ladybugs or predatory wasps to control aphids or encouraging certain bird species that prey on squirrels or rabbits or cabbage worms.

5. Chemical Control

Chemical control of pests, does include organic and natural pest control products. There are a lot of different commercial products and home remedies that can help control all kinds of pests around your garden and are too numerous to mention here. Also, because of your unique garden climate and local laws regulating what's available to use in your garden, you will need to consult your local nursery, master gardener, or other garden professional when opting to use these products.

When choosing any of these pest control options or categories, it's good sense to wear gloves and any other protective gear due to any unforeseen reactions or interactions.

PRUNING

Pruning is the removal of plant stems, branches, leaves, or roots to remove dead or diseased tissues, encourage proper growth, and influence plant shape.

Prune your plants to not only keep them shaped and formed correctly in your garden but also to keep them healthy by removing any dead tissue and improving air circulation to keep insects and diseases to a minimum.

To prune your plants and flowers, you will need three basic hand tools: hand shears, loppers, and a pruning saw. With these, you will also need to have a bucket or wheelbarrow to put your debris into, a rake, and a broom to help with cleanup. Check out the photos on page 74 to see examples of hand pruning tools and what size of cut you can use them for.

The first thing to know when pruning plants is that you want to make the correct cut using the right technique. Cut stems at a 45° angle about ¼ to ½ inch (0.6 to 1.3 cm) above a bud or the point of attachment of that stem to the main branch of the plant. Make the cleanest cut you can with

Pruning shears are great for cutting branches or stems up to 1 inch (2.5 cm) in diameter.

your pruning tools so there is not tearing or ripping of plant tissue. A clean cut will ensure fast healing and reduce the chance of bacterial or fungal infections later.

For any hand shear or lopper tools, we recommend you use a bypass-operated tool. This is not only because they operate very similarly to scissors to give you a very clean cut, but they also are much gentler when cutting plant tissue than an anvil-operated tool. Anvil pruners and loppers cut away plant tissue with a combination of a knife on a chopping block which partially crushes plant stem tissue in the process of cutting. This makes for more damage to the cut area of the plant when pruned, and more healing is needed.

To keep your plants healthy, you need to know how to prune your plants, what cuts to make, and why you are making those cuts. You should also understand why you make any cuts on your plants in the first place. Our rule of thumb on pruning is "if you don't know why you are pruning any plant, then don't prune it at all; leave it alone until you know why you would make that or any other cut." Also, don't prune and remove more than one-third of a plant's total mass at any one time or during one full year. This is so the plant isn't put under the stress of having a large amount of its total growth removed all at once. Some plants will react favorably to this, and others will not. It is important to know for each plant. If you don't know, then don't prune the plant.

It sounds like obvious advice, but it might surprise you to know how many people prune plants every year and don't even really know why they are pruning or how to actually prune them correctly. Let's first talk about why we prune for health first, then we'll introduce two basic pruning cuts, and finally we'll get into some other reasons you should prune your plants.

Pruning loppers are great for cutting branches up to 2.5 inches (6.4 cm) in diameter.

Pruning for Plant Health

To prune for your plant's health, you should prune:

- To remove any dead or diseased wood or tissues

- To remove rubbing branches and decrease the chance of crossing branches that can turn into rubbing branches in the future

- To then prune for a healthy shape and normal growth where your plant can remain healthy with spacing and airflow around it

Pruning for health is almost a no-brainer. It seems easy, and it is. It just takes some time to get oriented with your plants to see what they need and how to go about getting them there. Fun, right? A quick word here on why we would remove dead, diseased, rubbing branches or stems, and roots. Any dead wood can become habitat for pests and a possible disease breeding ground where it can then spread out to other vulnerable parts of your plant. You also want to remove any rubbing branches or crossing branches that could later

ECO-FRIENDLY PEST CONTROL METHODS

Evidence of slug damage as indicated by the small holes in plant leaves.

- DIY Soap Spray (pest control): Mix water with any kind of regular liquid dish soap at a ratio of 10 parts water to 1 part soap into a misting spray bottle. Great for controlling aphids, whiteflies, thrips, earwigs, and other soft-bodied insects. This can be applied around your garden and is safe to handle, along with using around children, pets, and other people. Test spray a small area of a plant before using on the entire plant to ensure there are no sensitivities.

- Cayenne Pepper (repellant): Either sprinkled in strategic locations every couple of days or incorporated into other gel or spray concoctions, cayenne pepper can repel many different garden pests, including aphids, squirrels, deer, rabbits, beetles, leaf-hoppers, and more. There are also commercial brands of pepper sprays.

- Peppermint (repellant): As an oil or infusion spray, peppermint works great to repel many common garden pests like aphids, ants, and others. You can mix a few drops of peppermint oil with water or purchase a commercial preparation.

- Diatomaceous Earth, or DE (control/prevention): These crushed fossilized aquatic organisms are made of silica with very sharp edges. When applied along garden bed borders or in circles around plants and pots, DE can control and prevent slug and snail damage on your plants. You'll need to reapply after rain.

become diseased due to having open rubbed wounds. Think about pruning as a cyclical pattern. If plants are pruned correctly over time and kept healthy with proper spacing and encouraged to grow according to their natural growth pattern, then the possibility of any rubbing or crossing branches is very low, which also makes dead and diseased tissues less of a possibility later on. If proper pruning doesn't happen for a plant, then the crossing and rubbing can happen more frequently, increasing the incidence of disease.

Two Basic Pruning Cuts

We'd like to introduce you to two basic pruning cuts: thinning cuts and heading back cuts.

- **Thinning cuts** are just as the name sounds. With this type of pruning, you are thinning out a plant to open up space between the stems or branches. Thinning cuts are industry defined by where you make your cut. Each cut is made at the point of attachment to the larger stem. This means you wouldn't cut a stem or branch in the middle or just above a bud or a leaf, but instead you cut it all the way back to where it originates off a larger stem. This also means you would not leave any part of that stem or branch behind after the cut. Thinning cuts give a plant a very natural shape and look informal with no clear lines.

Pruning saws are great for cutting branches up to 7 inches (17.8 cm) in diameter.

HOW TO MAKE A PROPER PRUNING CUT, SHOWN HERE ON A ROSE STEM

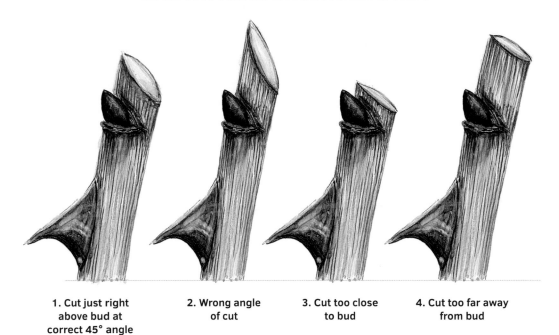

1. Cut just right above bud at correct 45° angle

2. Wrong angle of cut

3. Cut too close to bud

4. Cut too far away from bud

NOTICE THE DIFFERENCE OF WHERE THE THINNING CUTS WERE MADE BETWEEN THE BEFORE-AND-AFTER EXAMPLES

Before Thinning Cuts

Where thinning cuts were made

After Thinning Cuts

BEFORE-AND-AFTER EXAMPLES OF HOW TO MAKE HEADING BACK CUTS ON ANY PLANT

Before Heading Back Cuts

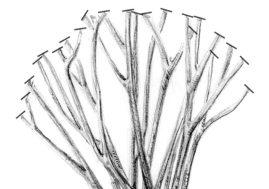

Where heading back cuts were made

After Heading Back Cuts

- The other cuts to make are called **heading back cuts**, and these can be thought of as the opposite of thinning cuts. Instead of cutting at a branch juncture, you make your cuts in the middle of a stem or branch, just above a bud or leaf. There is part of that stem or branch still attached to the plant after the cut. You have seen heading back cuts if you've seen shrubs that are formally shaped into balls, squares, rectangles, and other geometric shapes, including tightly pruned hedges.

More Reasons to Prune

Besides pruning for overall health, there are other reasons to prune plants. You might want to truly shape a plant a certain way to enhance your garden and to increase your home's curb appeal. Pruning is also done to reinvigorate or rejuvenate an older plant to reset it to flower more or to get it reestablished in form or shape to fit better with your garden vision. This can be an extreme form of pruning, but it is sometimes necessary. By removing more than one-third of the plant's stems and leaves, you are telling it to stop what it's doing and start generating new growth immediately. Always be careful to

EXAMPLE OF A PLANT BEFORE AND AFTER IT WAS PRUNED TO REJUVENATE IT

Before Rejuvenating Cuts

After Rejuvenating Cuts

research if a plant you want to prune hard to rejuvenate is known to react well to this type of pruning. Some plants, like English laurel and lilacs, will react well; others such as Skimmia will start to decline and eventually die. Remember that when pruning a plant, removing up to one-third of the plant material is about the most you want to prune away at any one time. Any more and you are going to increase the level of stress, lowering the plant's ability to resist pests and diseases.

Some gardeners prune to create more space in their garden for other plants to then be planted and/or grow into. There is also pruning to increase airflow circulation to keep moisture low and control diseases and pest infestations.

WEEDING

A weed is generally defined as any plant that isn't supposed to be in your garden. This could include herbaceous, deciduous, or evergreen plants. Basically, almost any type of plant could be considered a weed. Learning how to prevent and manage garden weeds is usually at the top of most gardeners' lists.

Weeds can grow almost any time of year, unless the ground is frozen, and can be found as annuals, biennials, or perennials. Because of this, weeds can be a bit challenging to control. Weeds are the jerks of the garden because they just keep regrowing no matter how many times you pull them out. They cause frustration to gardeners around the world because they can grow in any climate, in any garden, and at any time of year.

Weeds can be invasive or noninvasive, depending on if they are naturally occurring in the area or not. Noninvasive species of weeds can be any type of plant that is native to the area or climate but is just unwanted nonetheless.

Invasive species of weeds are those that have been introduced to an area where they are not previously known to grow. Invasive weeds generally take over and compete with native plants for access to resources such as water, space, soil, and sunlight. They crowd out the native plants and essentially steal all their nutrients, leading to disease or death if uncontrolled.

BAD PRUNING PRACTICES TO AVOID

- Don't use dirty or neglected tools. Clean and sharpen your pruning tools on a regular basis so as not to spread any diseases and to make the best cuts you can.

- Don't leave extra stem or branch tissue when pruning. This is mainly for thinning cuts and is referred to as leaving a "stub" or making stub cuts. Always prune back to a stem's point of attachment. Stubs take longer for the plant to heal and can make it easier for insects and diseases to make a home.

- Don't prune a plant during dry conditions or when temperatures are excessively high. During these conditions, postpone pruning until the plant can be better hydrated and the temperature is milder so as not to add more stress to the plant.

- Double check to make sure a plant can be pruned into a hedge, ball, or other type of formal shape. Not all plants are created equal, and pruning certain plants in these ways can kill them.

Make sure you remove the whole root of any weed. Sometimes you need to dig it out using a trowel.

An important part of maintaining your garden and caring for your plants is weed prevention and control. Control is aimed at stopping the spread of weeds already present. Prevention is stopping any germination or presence of weeds before they become established and then need control. Weed prevention is preferred, whenever possible in your garden, and can help limit larger issues later on. Once weeds are established, they will take more energy to eliminate and could lead to possible technologies that we might not be comfortable using, like chemical controls.

Everyone wants a quick fix for controlling weeds, but the truth is, to get a grip on weeds, diligence and patience are the best tools. Weeds like to take advantage of any open areas of space, and unfortunately, they grow much faster and far more efficiently than most garden plants. Weeds readily adapt to low or high water, light, and nutrient levels.

When you anticipate weeds, you can stay ahead of and prevent them. Luckily, most of the methods of weed prevention come back to "right plant, right place," as well as a few other garden care methods. These weed-prevention strategies include mulching, correctly spacing plants for their mature size, not over- or underwatering, providing enough sunlight or shade, and growing your plants in the right soil. Also, if you have weeds in other parts of your garden, be sure to remove them before their flowers are fertilized. After this point, they will produce seeds that can then spread to other areas of

your garden, which would be bad. So, overall, knowing your plant's care needs is your best weapon to prevent weeds in your garden.

When prevention isn't possible and you already have established weeds in your garden, control is you best next weapon against weeds. Control includes removing weeds by hand, using hand tools, or using a rototiller. Other ways to control weeds are squelching, or suffocating, weeds with barriers like mulch, landscape fabric, cardboard, burlap, and even sometimes black plastic. This suffocation method of control is usually performed once, often lasting for many years.

Removing weeds by hand is old-fashioned but works really well. Plus, it's great exercise. To fully remove any weed, especially aggressive ones, you need to dig and remove the whole plant from the soil. This includes all the roots. Be sure to not leave any root behind because more aggressive weeds can regrow from even small pieces. You should always try to remove weeds before they have a chance to grow and disperse their seeds. If seeds are spread in your garden, you could be hand weeding or trying to control a weed anywhere from 5 years up to 50 years (or even longer), depending on that weed and how long its seed stays viable in the environment (again, they're jerks).

Mulching on a regular basis, and even sheet mulching, is another great way to control weeds in your garden. Creating this barrier over the top of your garden soil makes it harder for weed seeds to germinate. This is due to the blockage of water and sunlight, along with the creation of temperature differences, making it an unsuitable environment for weeds. Remember to use mulch at least 2 to 4 inches (5 to 10 cm) thick. And that would go on top of any cardboard, newspaper, or any other sheet mulching material.

Besides the above physical control methods, there are other options using various vinegar mixtures to control weeds. These are sold by nurseries and online, but you can also make your own mixture at home. There are other chemicals out there that will control weeds, but always use caution when handling and using any chemical and always read the label before opening any chemical container. The label is the law.

The tools you use to remove weeds from your garden depend on what weeds need to be removed and how large the area is. For small areas with just a few weeds, a hand trowel works well. For larger areas, use a hula hoe and rake for shallow-rooted weeds. If you have any weeds that have deep growing roots, a shovel and pitchfork work well. Deeper and more extensively rooted weeds need not just their immediate roots, crown, and leaves removed; you also might need to remove any underground stems or roots growing out further so they don't keep coming back. The shovel and pitchfork can help dig and loosen surrounding soil from the weed and expose those other stems and roots.

Weeds can be fast growing and take over large areas of your garden. Weed your garden regularly and remove any unwanted plants because they will compete with your garden plants for growing space, water, sunlight, and nutrients. Every region of the globe has its own set of problematic weeds. Get familiar with weeds common in your region and the best ways to control or remove them.

Use a hula hoe to remove shallow-rooted weeds over a large area or in tight spaces.

below ground care

Most of the aboveground care directly relates to a plant's belowground care. They are intertwined and influence each other, with below ground being just as important as above ground. Belowground care focuses largely on maintaining healthy soil and plant roots. The main components of belowground plant care are composting, fertilizing, soil building, and watering. Let's discuss them each in turn.

Waste not everything that comes out of your kitchen. Some of your food scraps can be composted into making healthier garden soil.

COMPOSTING

Composting is the collecting and breaking down of different sources of organic matter, including noninvasive plant stems and leaves, kitchen vegetable trimmings, leaves, and other materials. After breaking down into a soil-like material called compost, it can then be mixed back into your existing garden soil to add nutrients and enhance soil structure for plant root development, water availability, and drainage.

Composting is important not only to improve your garden's health but also because it helps recycle garden and kitchen debris that would otherwise be disposed of at local landfills. If garden debris and kitchen materials are recycled by private or public entities, this is still better than being added to landfill sites; but it also adds to transportation emissions in your area that can impact air quality and your community's environment. Composting at home is a fun and rewarding experience if you have the option and time to do it.

Where to Compost

When siting a compost area or bin in your garden, look for an area that is level and away from your home or any buildings and has good drainage. If you live in a cooler climate, your compost bin can have a mostly to full-sun exposure. If you live in a warmer climate, you can locate your compost bin in a full-sun exposure, knowing that this will hasten the breakdown of your material. Also, the warmer temperature and faster decomposing of material mean it can dry out fast and you might need to add some water so the decomposing organisms don't die.

WHAT TO COMPOST

There are many different items that can be tossed into a compost pile or bin and others that should be left out. Ideally, your pile should consist of a mixture of ingredients, some fresh and green and others brown and dry. Pile them up and let the microbes do their thing.

To Compost

- Pruned stems and leaves from garden plants (hardwood stems larger than ¼ inch [0.6 cm] will slow down decomposition)

- Any noninvasive weed tissues

- Kitchen vegetable scraps and fruit rinds, coffee grounds, unbleached paper products

- Lawn clippings, if you have a lawn or grass areas (only add if you don't use a typical weed-and-feed fertilizer)

- Fall leaves

- Herbivore manure (horse, cow, sheep, rabbit)

Not to Compost

- Any lawn clippings from grass areas where synthetic weed-and-feed fertilizer has been applied

- Meat or bones of any kind

- Sauces or dressings, as these can attract rodents

- Food scraps covered with cooking oil

- Pet waste

Turning the Pile

In general, you want to turn/mix your compost pile every 2 to 3 weeks at a minimum in cooler climates because you need to let all the organisms decompose the material. If you turn material more frequently than every 2 to 3 weeks, it will take longer for all the material to break down to usable material. If you live in a warmer climate, you should be able to rotate every 1½ to 3 weeks or sooner, depending on how fast your material breaks down.

Once your compost is broken down into a soil-like textured material, similar to sand or finer, you can then add it back into your garden to help feed your plants and soil.

Make sure you mix your compost every 2 weeks or so.

FERTILIZING

There are entire college courses on nothing but fertilizing. It's a complicated subject. Here, we'd like to offer you some basic information about fertilizing your plants and flowers for better performance.

What Is a Fertilizer?

Fertilizer is a granular or liquid substance added to the soil or plant foliage to increase available nutrients for better plant health. Fertilizers can be natural or man-made.

Fertilizers provide essential nutrients that native garden soil may not be able to provide on its own. Like us, plants need essential nutrients to stay healthy, and those nutrients need to be replenished on a regular basis. This could be every 2 weeks or every 2 months, depending on the fertilizer used and the quality of your native soil. If nutrients are depleted and not replenished regularly, your plants start to develop yellowing or discolored leaves, less overall growth, and fewer and smaller flowers. A fertilizer's physical characteristics (powder, granular, manure, or liquid) impact how it's used and applied.

Some fertilizers, like water-soluble or liquid fertilizers, can be spread directly over the top of your garden soil where regular watering and gravity move the nutrients down

WHAT IS N-P-K?

These three letters represent the percentage of available nitrogen, phosphorus, and potassium (K is the chemical symbol for potassium) in a fertilizer product. A well balanced organic fertilizer with an N-P-K of 4-3-3 will help plants maintain their health, with a slightly higher level of nitrogen to encourage more leaf growth than roots or flowers.

into the soil. Other fertilizers are mixed into your garden soil before planting or worked into the soil after plants are established. These fertilizers are usually activated by moisture, so read the label of any product you are using so you know how it is to be applied.

Types of Fertilizers

Examples of easy-to-apply fertilizers are different kinds of manures (e.g., chicken, cow, horse) that you mix with existing garden soil. These can be slow to break down, and the released nutrients are available to plants over a long period of time. Another example of fertilizers are different kinds of composts. These can be spread right over the top of your garden soil near plants or mixed in with a pitchfork or shovel. There are also companies that produce organically sourced and processed granular fertilizers from a mixture of natural ingredients. These products not only supply nutrients to your plants but also build soil structure, along with creating a beneficial soil environment for microorganisms and other soil animals to thrive. You can find our favorite sources for garden fertilizer in Appendix 2 in the back of this book to learn more.

Which Fertilizer Is Best?

Briefly, when you are choosing a fertilizer for flowering plants, look for one with equal amounts of the three main nutrients. These numbers represent the available nitrogen, phosphorus, and potassium (N-P-K) in that specific fertilizer. It is important to note that the percentages of these nutrients are what is available to plants in this product. If you have a balanced fertilizer with an N P K of 4-4-4 or 12-12-12, then when you use this fertilizer, you get equal parts nitrogen, phosphorus, and potassium. It's important to note that with a balanced fertilizer like this, your plants will be encouraged equally to grow more leaves (nitrogen), produce more roots and flowers (phosphorous), and increase plant vigor (potassium). There are other fertilizers produced and sold to encourage plants to grow and develop in specific ways. For example, some

Naturally sourced fertilizer, like in this photo, provides the needed N-P-K and other nutrients your plants need to thrive.

gardeners use fertilizers higher in phosphorous to encourage flowering. Other gardeners use a fertilizer with a higher percentage of phosphorus to encourage root growth for plants to become established faster in their garden. And then even other gardeners will choose to use a higher percentage of nitrogen to give their plants a flush of new leaf and stem growth, which can be advantageous when a plant has been heavily pruned or is trying to recover from some pest or storm damage. While these unbalanced fertilizers are tempting to use to get specific results, they can result in unbalanced growth of your plants, where forcing them to grow specific ways will create unneeded stresses. Therefore, using a balanced fertilizer is best for new gardeners.

How to Apply Fertilizer

You will need rubber gloves, some measuring equipment (if you are mixing anything), and a spreader, broadcaster, or a slotted hole cap to sprinkle the fertilizer with. It really depends on the fertilizer itself and how it is labeled to be applied. *Always* follow the label.

Since how to actually use and apply fertilizer is so subjective, we will give you some general guidelines so you can then have a better idea of what you could encounter. Numerous companies offer organic fertilizers to add directly to your planting hole for individual plants or to be mixed into whole garden beds before planting new plants. They are usually a dry granular or ground pellet product in which all or part of the package is used, depending on the size of your garden bed. They use dry weight or volume measurements to be mixed and used, so make sure to purchase measuring cups, spoons, and maybe even a small weight scale if you are planning on using these fertilizers.

To err on the side of caution, always mix on the lower side so you don't burn or otherwise harm your garden plants or soil. And always wear some kind of gloves, usually moisture-proof.

SOIL BUILDING AND AMENDING

We promised several times throughout this book that we would share with you a great way to "fix" soil texture if it's less than ideal. This is where we do just that. Soil building and amending involves improving your garden soil, and here's why it's important.

Common reasons to amend your garden soil are:

- To improve drainage

- To increase water holding and nutrient holding capacity

- To lessen compaction

- To enhance soil structure (or the assembly of sand, silt, and clay particles)

Amending your soil is important because not all soils are created equal. In different regions, counties, provinces, and even cities and neighborhoods, soil can be very different in how fast or slow it drains, how compacted it is, its overall texture, the level of nutrients available to plants, and many other things. It's actually quite interesting to think about all the different variations of soil there are and how plants have either adapted or suffered to keep growing in them.

When you are modifying your soil, you will most likely need a hand trowel for small garden areas or containers, a shovel and a pitchfork for larger garden areas, and possibly a wheelbarrow if you need to move large amounts of material into or out of a garden area.

Here are examples of how to improve your garden soil using different materials for each of the common reasons already mentioned. For easy application of these examples, try adding 1 to 2 inches (2.5 to 5 cm) thick of any material to the top of your garden's soil and then thoroughly mixing it in. If you need to add more material after this, add more material 1 inch (2.5 cm) at a time.

left First, prepare your planting hole by digging it to the correct size and depth. **top right** Next, add compost then mix it with the soil from the planting hole. **bottom right** Now add your new plant to the planting hole and backfill with mixed soil.

To improve slow drainage, increase water and nutrient holding capacity, and decrease compaction: For fast results, add compost to your soil and mix in as thoroughly as possible around your plants, being sure not to disturb plant roots by not getting too close. Once mixed to your liking, level the soil and replace any mulch you had over the top of your soil. If your soil already has a good amount of compost in it, try adding plain sand instead for better drainage.

To decrease fast drainage: Adding compost works here, too; and it's our go-to. Compost is a miracle material; just be sure your plants won't be adversely affected by the specific compost you use. Also, to slow down water entering your fast draining soil, adding mulch over the top of your soil is a good option. This pairing of adding compost into your soil and spreading mulch over the top of your soil is a great solution to slowing down your garden soil's water drainage. Always do your homework to know your plants' needs before making any changes to your garden soil.

WATERING

All plants need water, and some need more than others. To regulate functions like respiration, nutrient, and energy movement, and even cellular integrity, water literally makes our world a greener place.

Watering a plant means applying water to garden soil to thoroughly saturate it. That water is then available for plant uptake. Refer back to Chapter 1 for more details on why plants need water.

A watering wand is an extended watering nozzle that attaches to your hose and is great for hard-to-reach places to water.

A watering can is a carrying container to bring water to plants not accessible by hose.

A hand nozzle sprayer attaches directly to your hose to quickly water plants close by.

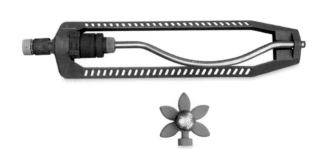

A sprinkler attaches directly to your hose and is used to water large areas at once.

THE IMPORTANCE OF WATERING PLANTS IN THE EARLY MORNING

The morning is the best time of day to water your plants for a couple of reasons:

- Lower temperatures mean less water lost to evaporation.

- Plants aren't using as much water as compared to afternoon.

- Foliage can dry before nightfall when pests and diseases more readily take hold.

In the early morning, plants are less stressed and have low respiration rates, so watering during this time of day is great for them. The best times are in the very early morning at sunrise or just before the sun comes up, or during the late afternoon or early evening.

You have to water more and longer during the hottest time of the day because the water is evaporating from the plant and the soil at a faster rate. This can also lead to underwatering your plants. Watering during the hottest time of day is inefficient.

Instead of going over again the importance of watering, let's talk about some technique and steps to keep your plants hydrated. Make sure to water the soil areas around the base of plants and where their roots are likely growing. Watering your plants, leaves, stems, and flowers might seem like a good idea, but it is a very inefficient way to water your plants. This is because a plant takes up a large majority of water through its roots, so watering the top of the plant lets water evaporate before it has a chance to enter the roots. Setting up ground-level soaker hoses or a drip system in your garden is more efficient, and you get the water right where it needs to go. As you water your plants, make sure to use low water pressure or a low setting on your nozzle so the soil doesn't wash away and the water doesn't run off. The closer your watering is to natural rainfall, the better. With too high of a water pressure, you can move soil around your plants to destabilize them and also expose plant roots.

Make sure to not over- or underwater your plants because either of these can lead to other problems. This means you will need to know your plants' and plant groupings' watering needs. An easy way to avoid over- or underwatering is to place your plants in groups that have the same or similar water needs.

Monitor your plants on a regular basis, especially during the hottest times of the year, and keep them on a regular watering schedule. This can be by regularly scheduled hand watering or with an automated system. There are simple or complex watering timers you can use that have soil moisture sensors to help your plants receive consistent irrigation without being overwatered too.

Deep watering can help your plants grow deeper roots so they can better handle future drought conditions. Plus, it's a more efficient use of water.

When it comes to hand watering, getting water down to your plant roots will most likely take more than one pass with your watering nozzle or rain wand. A good approach is to water each plant with a watering pass, then make another pass applying the same amount of water again. Multiple passes allow the water to soak in deep.

ECO-FRIENDLY TIP: EAT YOUR WEEDS, SERIOUSLY

Yes, we are saying you can eat your weeds as part of your weed-control strategy. Now, you can't eat all of them; and always exercise caution before consuming plants. But there are a few common garden weeds that are edible:

- Dandelions—The leaves can be included in your salad, and roots can be cooked.

- Nettles—They can be included in your soups, or the leaves can be used in other ways. (Always be careful when harvesting. Wear gloves.)

- Purslane—All plant parts are considered edible for various dishes.

correct

above The correct way to water is down at the soil level so you don't waste any water. **right** The incorrect way to water is to spray over the top of the plant, wasting water on plant foliage.

incorrect

the essentials of care

Caring for your garden from season to season and from year to year is only part of your gardening journey. You have the basics of what you need to do for both above- and belowground care, along with the steps to get it done. Also, seeing how each of these can influence and impact the others opens your gardening experience. Mulching correctly helps not only to keep moisture in the soil longer but also with soil health and better nutrient availability. Amending your garden soil with compost, sand, clay, or other materials also improves nutrient availability.

Great garden care leads to beautiful and healthy plants and flowers from season to season.

In Chapter 6, we dive into some common garden problems that many gardeners have to deal with. Whether you have a couple of plants in pots or a vast landscape that extends into the back 40, these problems will pop up. We are going to give you easy ways to take care of them to keep your garden looking gorgeous. "You're gorgeous, darling! Gorgeous!"

KEY TAKEAWAYS FROM THIS CHAPTER

- Plants need care both above ground where they are visible and below ground where their roots are located.

- Mulching above ground helps below ground, too, by insulating plant roots, retaining moisture, and much more.

- Aboveground garden care directly affects and benefits belowground plant health, and vice versa.

DIG DEEPER

As a reminder, learn how to spread mulch correctly around your plants in Chapter 5 of the Bonus Companion Guide. Check it out at spokengarden.com/ftgbonusguide.

Common Garden Problems You Will Run Into (and how to avoid them)

Plants go through cycles and stress just like we do. Plants can experience stress due to extremes of water, temperature, changing soil conditions, wildlife habits, and even from human actions. Add in what the current health of the plant is at the time of the stress and it can get really interesting.

Learning to care for your own plants and flowers is such a rewarding experience. Unfortunately, that sense of accomplishment can be destroyed in a matter of minutes. The reality is, each gardener will run into a variety of challenges at some point in their gardening journey. Some of these problems will be within your control, and others will not. Let's dive into the frustrating subject of garden problems and how to fix them.

living problems

CRITTERS AND WILDLIFE MANAGEMENT

Wildlife, such as deer, squirrels, chipmunks, rabbits, and cats, can damage your garden in short order. They are considered animal pests because they are constantly eating and foraging. Some, like squirrels and chipmunks, hide and store their food around your garden, digging it up in the process. Deer and rabbits chew and eat your plants, even just trying them out to see if they like them. Cats are included in this list because they will lie down and roll over on plants, use your garden as a litter box, and mark their territory around various areas of your garden.

Deer have been known to feast on many garden flowers and plants.

You can prevent animals like these from damaging your plants, or at least make them less welcome, by using a couple of methods. First, deterrents—such as pepper flakes, cat or dog urine, and cat or dog hair from your vacuum cleaner or brushes—can discourage some animals. Physical barriers, like wire cages or fencing, can also keep them from entering your garden. Another option is to plant deer-resistant plants around your yard, such as rosemary, mint, daffodils, and alliums (onions and garlic), to name just a few. There are traps or baits to lure animals away or into cages to be relocated but only by trained professionals. Do not attempt to do this yourself. Most states have laws against private homeowners baiting or trapping animals. Whatever method you choose, make sure it won't harm wildlife with toxins or chemicals or contain any lethal substances. The idea is to deter them or keep them out, not to kill them.

SQUIRRELS:
Love Them, But What a Mess.

Squirrels are lovable garden critters that add energy to any garden. They are fun to watch as they run around. Unfortunately, these small rodents can also wreak havoc on your plants and garden beds.

Squirrels constantly scavenge. They are always on the lookout for sources of food, including bird-seed, pinecones, fruit, flowers, berries, and more. If they can't find these in or around your garden *and* you don't supply them with copious amounts of seed, nuts, suet, and other food sources, they lay waste to your garden without abandon, eating anything they can.

Another characteristic displayed by most squirrels is to find spots to bury their food to store it for later. Their tiny paws can rip up containers, garden beds, and other areas in seconds as they dig their tiny holes. They also dig up and eat garden bulbs, especially tulips and crocuses. Luckily, they will stay away from daffodils, alliums, and hyacinths.

Squirrels are fun to have around, but you need to take precautions. Eco-friendly deterrents such as pepper spray or physical barriers like chicken wire could keep them away from certain plants. Also, you may need to cover certain bulbs through the fall and winter months to deter these pesky pests.

Whether you want squirrels around or not, they will most likely show up if you live where they live; so you might as well learn how to coexist with them as best as you can.

OTHER PLANTS

Even with the best intentions of most gardeners, placing plants in their gardens without regard to their mature size can have some dire consequences that create more work and headaches later. As your garden grows and matures, your plants and flowers will also grow to fill in spaces, create shapes with their natural form, and expand into areas you might or might not have intended them to. A good example is when a plant near a walking path or just to the side of a home entrance starts to grow into the handrails or across the foot traffic path. These areas need to be kept clear for regular use. Once plants start to grow into these areas, it condenses the space available for others to occupy. The solution is to shape and prune these plants to keep the areas open.

Plants also grow up against buildings, creating an access issue for maintaining or repairing the building. Also, they can provide nesting areas for rats, mice, and other critters you don't want nesting on or next to your building. Spacing can also influence disease and pest problems.

Not only can plants grow to encroach on walkways and buildings, but they can grow into each other, too. Yes, you guessed it. Plants begin competing with other plants for resources. In addition, these dense plantings create low air circulation areas, leading to possible pests and diseases.

One other thing can happen when plants grow larger than you want them to. Unintended visual blockages that you can't see around or over create a safety issue. Blind spots are a real hazard and are usually solved permanently by full removal of that plant as it gets older.

As you now know from Chapter 2, spacing your plants correctly is very important when designing a garden. Avoid these aforementioned problems by spacing plants correctly every time you plant something new in your garden.

Solution Using Eco-friendly Methods

- If plantings become too dense, remove plants and place them in another location in your garden or gift them to another gardener.

- Another solution to dense plantings can be to prune certain plants back to a decent size so they temporarily don't grow into each other. This is only a short-term solution, though.

When plants grow into the walkway to change normal traffic patterns, it's time to open back up the walkway by pruning.

PESTS

Garden pests come in all shapes and sizes all over the world. Within every region and climate, specific garden pests exist—and there are too many to really mention in this book. As you now know after reading in Chapter 5, you can prevent and control pests using certain prevention and control methods. So, let's talk about a few specific visitors who might show up in your garden and cause problems at some point: slugs, aphids, and weevils. It's really nothing you did wrong. They are true opportunists who take the easy way to enter, nest, feed, and reproduce, all while you are completely unaware.

Slugs can cause major plant damage. Either follow their trail any time of day or try to catch them in the act in the very early morning.

Aphids are active during the day, and you can find them easily in your garden by looking for shriveled, crinkled, or even rolled down plant leaves. The leaves can also look a little wavy, slightly discolored, or a little smaller than the surrounding healthy leaves. You might be able to spot aphids on your plant's stems when they first arrive, but they mostly like to hang out on the underside of your plant's leaves. They can be many different colors and are very visible with the naked eye, with their six legs and a three-sectioned body. The back section is larger than the front. Aphids feed by sticking their needle mouths into the leaf or stem tissues to suck out the inside. This, you can imagine, is devastating to any plant and renders it stunted and disfigured.

Slugs and weevils both feed at night, so unless you are out in your garden with a flashlight looking for them (which some gardeners do), you will only see their damage. Slugs will leave a slime trail that you can follow. You'll often spot them near leaves and stems of soft-tissue plants, like coleus or hosta. Weevils will come up from the ground to put notches in such plant leaves as rhododendrons, viburnum, Aronia, and others. These kinds of stress on a plant can lead to further problems down the road by hurting the plant's ability to photosynthesize or function for healthy growth and flowering. The plant is losing its ability to turn sunlight into usable energy, and if the insects and slugs go unchecked, this will lead to plant death.

Aphids, being the opportunists they are, get drawn to plants that show some kind of stress. This is because these plants have lower defenses (stressed) and are much more susceptible to the aphid's attack. So, the easiest way to prevent aphids is to care for your plants and keep their stress low. Keep plants watered, fertilized, pruned, mulched, and in the right sunlight conditions.

Unwanted plants in your garden, or weeds, can be anywhere and can sometimes surprise you.

Slug control uses different naturally sourced deterrents that you sprinkle or cast around plants to create a physical barrier that they will not cross. These need to be re-done every 2+ weeks.

Weevil damage is the one of the easiest to solve. Simply make sure that your plants don't have any leaves touching the ground, and if they do, prune them up so the weevils have a harder time finding leaves to chew on.

Insects and slugs can be some of the worst garden pests out there, but other invasive and aggressively growing plants are also pretty bad and hard to keep out of your garden. Weeds, also known as common plant pests, will also show up when garden conditions are perfect for them to germinate and grow. Chapter 5 mentions weed prevention and control for you to reference.

DISEASES

Plant diseases are caused by bacteria, fungus, and viruses that infect plant tissues. This group is responsible for the root and stem rots, blights, and other common diseases of plants. As they spread, bacteria and fungi destroy or physically change a plant with their reproductive or fruiting bodies. As a result, the plant tissue turns brown, black, red, yellow, orange, or other colors and can no longer photosynthesize. This can starve a plant. Plant tissue that can be invaded by bacteria and fungi includes the leaves, stems, flowers, and roots. Viruses replicate themselves on a genetic level that ends up disfiguring plants, seen in oddly deformed leaf or stem shapes.

Powdery mildew, as seen on this azalea, thrives under a cool, wet, and dry warm cycle of weather.

It's important to know what damage these diseases can inflict on your garden plants because you can prevent most of them from occurring. These diseases mostly gain a foothold when they break through cell walls in susceptible plants, but most plants have built-in defenses. When plants are stressed and can't fight off these infections, that is when you will see these diseases.

Unless your garden plant is susceptible to a specific disease, you need to make sure to keep it healthy and happy. A healthy plant will have a much lower possibility of infection than a stressed or damaged plant. There are many different organic bacterial and fungal sprays you can make to control infections. Viral infections are almost impossible to treat because they are on a genetic level. Your best bet is to find plants that are resistant to any local viruses in your area.

nonliving problems

Nonliving plant problems, also called abiotic stressors, are caused by situations other than living organisms. Relating to sunlight, nutrients, and more, these problems stem from issues that you can usually prevent.

DRAINAGE

Situations like this not only get your feet wet but can also eventually drown your plants.

The movement of water through, over, and around your garden soil is very important for the health of your plants, your property value and curb appeal, and your own sanity. When that movement stops or is inhibited, that is when problems occur.

Common problems with drainage can be flooding, erosion, and dryness, which can all lead to plants being stressed in these extreme water-related environments.

Let's talk about a garden scenario where poor drainage exists in a garden bed. Water drains well off the property, and there is not any flooding in the garden. But the soil is actually too wet for most plants. Plants' roots are rotting, and their leaves are wilting. To improve the drainage of water in this garden bed, add compost and other organic material to the soil to improve the drainage. Our second example is a garden that has soil draining way too fast. By adding compost or other organic matter, this soil's drainage can be greatly improved so it drains more slowly. Whether the problem is too much drainage or too little, increased soil and organic matter (compost!) is the answer.

NUTRIENTS

Plants become nutrient deficient for a number of different reasons. There could be little to no nutrients in the soil. The soil pH may be too high or too low for the plant to take up the needed nutrients. Or perhaps the soil is holding on to the nutrients too tightly for the plant to get what it needs. There are other reasons for poor plant nutrition, but these are most common.

Nutrient deficiency can lead to even worse problems. With plants, different nutrient deficiencies can start a slow decline in the plant's ability to convert sunlight to usable energy, increase cellular degeneration, or weaken stems and roots and open them to bacterial and fungal infections. Even flower development and seed production are impacted by a plant not getting enough essential nutrients.

You can get ahead of any nutrient deficiency by regularly top-dressing your soil with a layer of compost up to 1 inch (2.5 cm) thick, usually every 6 months to a year. Also, start using an organic, slow-release fertilizer from a reputable source or manufacturer so you know that your plants are at least getting a balanced amount of nitrogen, phosphorus, and potassium (N-P-K). And do a soil test periodically to check your soil's pH and nutrient level availability.

A common sign of a nutrient deficiency is yellowing leaves due to nitrogen deficiency.

SUNLIGHT AND SHADE

Without the right amount of sunlight, plants will react by stretching their stems.

When plants don't get enough or too much sunlight, they start to grow in uncharacteristic ways. Just like us, plants need sunlight. The sunlight length, along with heat, helps trigger leaf and flower development, along with growth. Plants judge the time of year by temperatures and by the length of day to start and stop their growth cycles.

As a result, it's important that plants are placed in your garden to receive the right amount of light to stay healthy (back to Chapter 2 we go). Your garden will grow over time, and you need to be aware of your plants so they don't crowd or overgrow each other.

When planning and designing any garden, space your plants accordingly, so they have enough room to grow into their mature size (we sound like a broken record). Also, after planting, you can prune them or move them to take care of overcrowding.

ECO-FRIENDLY TIP:
PLANTS DON'T WASTE WATER, AND NEITHER SHOULD YOU

Plants use water efficiently to optimize their growth and reproduction. It just makes sense when they have a limited resource. Follow their example with these efficient watering tips:

- Deep water. This helps plants grow deeper roots by watering more infrequently.

- Plant more drought-tolerant plants. In general, these plants can tolerate less frequent watering.

- Set up an automated watering system. Install soaker hoses that connect to your hose and are timed to water at certain intervals.

- Catch rain using rain barrels.

UTILITIES

Around homes and gardens, there are various utility lines and pipes. Life would get ugly if we didn't have them, but most gardeners will tell you that they don't know where their utilities are. This is a problem.

Your garden plants might have already grown and covered them, and now you aren't sure where they are or how to get to them. A good example is when plants grow into or over-take utility boxes, cages, water line vaults, and even gas meters.

You may not know this, but it is your responsibility as the homeowner to keep these boxes and the areas around them clear and accessible at all times. Sure, we forget about these areas, and actually some of us would like our plants to grow large enough to hide or completely engulf these boxes because they could be considered "eyesores." This is where you can remove the plants that are there and replace them with smarter, more appropriate plants that won't overgrow where they were intended to grow—that's right, using "right plant, right place." Until you can replace the overgrown plants, keep the immediate area around the utilities clear and accessible for maintenance as it's needed. For specifics on utilities, you can call your city, county, or private provider to learn what they need for clearance. Normally, clearance around any utility should be a perimeter of 2 to 3 feet (0.6 to 0.9 m), and if anything is overhead, then those areas also need to be and stay clear around them.

Before you dig, you should know where all your pipes are located.

DIG DEEPER

To learn more about how to identify a few common nutrient deficiencies and how to treat them, visit our Bonus Companion Guide to dig deeper into plant nutrient deficiency. Check it out in Chapter 6 at spokengarden.com/ftgbonusguide.

problems happen

With any garden care routine, there will be problems. You can spend hours in your garden controlling aphids, preventing slugs, and deterring deer (and probably pulling weeds), but the reality is, they'll probably show up anyway. The goal is to always find an eco-friendly solution to your problem. Not only will you feel better, but you'll help support the environment and all the critters within it, too. Next up, it is time to put it all together with a glimpse into what garden care might look like throughout the year and the specific tasks you'll need to do during each season.

Plant problems come in all shapes and sizes, like this leaf damage by weevils.

KEY TAKEAWAYS FROM THIS CHAPTER:

- Even the cute and cuddly animals can wreak havoc on your garden.

- By giving your plants the right care and keeping them healthy, you can prevent many different pests and diseases from ever occurring.

- When problems do arise in your garden, you have many different options besides using chemicals, pesticides, or toxic substances to solve the problem.

Putting It All together

Through plant parts and the concept of "right plant, right place," you got to know plants better. Then by becoming familiar with how to plant different stages of plants and bulbs, along with learning how to care for your garden, you were able to start seeing some of the problems you'll encounter later. Now is your opportunity to start putting all this information together and setting it all into practice. But wait, there's more. We need to talk about the gardening seasons and how plants grow throughout them so you know what to expect in your garden year-round.

garden care through all four seasons

As you're becoming more familiar with your garden, you're also becoming more aware of its needs. You've now learned that your plants will need to be mulched, pruned, weeded, fertilized, and much more. Unfortunately, it's often confusing to first-time gardeners *when* each of these garden care tasks should be performed. Do they all happen at once? Are certain garden tasks performed before other tasks? In the section that follows, each season is broken down into the type of garden care that should be performed during that time.

Keep in mind that these seasonal tasks may vary a bit from year to year due to temperature changes in the environment, possible rainfall differences, or drought possibly affecting plants and causing them to react differently.

Primrose, a winter blooming plant, can be deadheaded to prolong how long it blooms.

WINTER

In the winter, the outside temperatures may be at or below freezing, depending on where you live. You will see shorter day lengths and thus less sunlight available for your garden. Above ground, many plants are dormant, meaning they are asleep through these colder months. However, some plants are still awake and will flower this time of year, like the hellebore and camellia. Overall, whether dormant or awake, plant roots continue to grow and breathe below ground and still need water and nutrients to survive.

Unless you live in a tropical climate, during the winter season, garden activity slows down; but your plant care focus should be on protection. This protection can come in the form of physical protection (from the cold weather) or nutritional protection (to keep plants healthy). For example, mulching is very important this time of year. Plants need their roots insulated from the cold, freezing temperatures. This can be done by making sure they have at least 2 to 4 inches (5 to 10 cm) of mulch over their roots in the planting beds. Also, you'll need to spread compost to build soil and add nutrients to the ground. This can be anywhere from ½ inch (1.3 cm) up to 2 inches (5 cm) over a planting bed. If you do spread compost in your garden beds and compost is not your mulch, then you will need to rake away any mulch material, like arborist chip or rock, to spread your compost and then rake the mulch back in and over the compost.

In addition, weeding will continue and is a form of protection because you need to control the growing space around the plant so it has more room to grow into in the spring season. (By the way, weeds never stop growing.) This can be hard because, during this time of year, the ground and garden soil can be frozen, making it extremely hard to pull any weeds out of the ground. You might be able to remove any weed stems and leaves, but the weeds' roots might not budge because they are interlocked with the frozen garden soil. If you need to weed during the winter, be sure to actually do your weeding when the ground isn't frozen or has thawed enough to be loosened by weeding tools and the whole plant, including roots, can be removed.

An alternative to physically weeding during the winter, and if your garden is in need of some new mulch, is to sheet mulch directly over any weeds and around your garden plants with cardboard or thick layers of newspaper. By doing this, you will cover the weeds so no light can reach them and they will eventually die because they will not be able to photosynthesize. By using cardboard or newspaper, you block sunlight long enough for weeds to die.

Another form of protection is physically moving your flowers in containers close to your house, your shed, an arbor, or some kind of structure that offers residual heat. In the extreme cases of very cold, icy temperatures, cover your plants with some type of burlap sheet, coffee bags, cardboard, or other type of biodegradable material to protect and insulate them. There is the practice of "heeling in" your plants in containers so their roots are not damaged during freezing temperatures and the extreme cold. This would be done by grouping your plants in any containers close together and then mounding woodchips or another type of mulch up to the edge of each pot in the group so that you can no longer see the pots and there is even a little mulch inside each pot but not touching or covering plant stems. You would leave each pot in this grouping until the threat of the extreme cold or freezing temperatures has passed. Then you could place each container where desired for the coming spring season.

SPRING

During the spring season, outside temperatures begin to rise and the days are getting longer. This means there is a lot more sunlight available for plants, stimulating their leaf and flower growth. Above ground, plant stems are growing as plants begin to wake up with this increase of sunlight causing flower buds to open. Below the ground level, plant roots continue to grow as stored energy from the winter is ready to be used for stem, leaf, and flower growth.

In addition, wildlife is mating and nesting. Plus, early pollinators are emerging. By planting pollinator-friendly flowers, you can encourage more pollinators to your yard.

During spring season, garden activity will begin to increase as the temperature and daylight length increase. It's time to anticipate the flush of new growth as plants wake up from the winter and set everything up for success. Overall, the key to spring season is planning.

Spring flowers, like this allium, attract many different pollinators, including bumblebees.

These summer-blooming crocosmia need little care besides staking their tall flower stems.

SUMMER

During the summer season, outside temperatures are really turning on the heat and day length has peaked. Our days are slowly getting shorter now. This also means your plants are in their high time, growing as tall and as fast as they can. Above ground, plant stems are still growing but also gaining some girth to support their ever-increasing flower numbers and weight. The number of flowers has grown exponentially, and so have all the pollinators who take advantage of those flowers. Below the ground level, plant roots, as usual, continue to grow, looking to take in more water and nutrients as the need is ever increasing.

During the summer season, garden activity will be at its height with the brightest colors and largest flowers your plants can produce. Oh, and the 90°F (32°C) heat is helping your sun-loving plants reach new heights of gorgeousness. Overall, the key to summer season is growth and lots of color.

PLANT GROWTH AND FLOWERING BY SEASON

Plant Name	Winter	Spring	Summer	Fall
Asters (P)	D ------------------------------►	G -------------------------------►	F ----------- ►	D ---------►
Black-Eyed Susan (Bl)	D ------------------------------►	G -------------------►	F ----------------------- ►	D -----------►
Chrysanthemum (P)	D ------------------------------►	G ----------------------------►	F -------------- ►	D ----►
Coneflower (P)	D -----------------►	G --►	F -------------------- ►	D ---------►
Cosmos (A)		S --- ► G -----------------►	F --- ►	Composted
Daffodil (B)	G --- ► F ---------------------- ►	D ---►		
Fuchsia (A/P)	Cutting	G ----------► F ------------------------------------ ►		Composted
Geranium (A)	Cutting/Seed	G -----------► F ------------------------------------ ►		Composted
Hellebore (P)	F ----------------------------- ►	D -----------------------------►	G ------------------ ►	F -- ►
Hosta (P)	D ------------------------------►	G ----------------------►	F ------------------------ ►	D ----►
Hydrangea (P)	D ►	G --------------------►	F ------------------------ ►	D ---------►
Lavender (P)	D ------------------------------►	G -----------------------►	F ---------------------- ►	D ----►
Pansies (A)		S -- ► G --------► F --- ►		Composted
Primroses (P)	G --- ► F ---------------------- ►	D --►		►
Tulip (B)	G - ► F ----------------- ►	D --►		►
Zinnia (A)		S --- ► G ------------► F ----------------------------------- ►		Composted

A = Annual	**D** = Dormant	**G** = Growing	**F** = Flowering	**S** = Seed Planting
P = Perennial	--► (Brown)	--► (Green)	--► (Pink)	--► (Yellow)
B = Bulb				
Bl = Biennial				

FALL

During the fall season, outside temperatures are still warm and just below that summer heat. But it's beginning to cool off sooner in the afternoons, and nighttime temperatures are reaching down with some frosty mornings. The day length is also getting noticeably much shorter, and plants have either stopped growing and flowering altogether or are in their final flowering push. Dormancy is right around the corner for many summer-flowering plants. Above ground, plants are losing their leaves, dropping flowers, and wondering where their fresh yearly mulch is to insulate them in the fast-approaching cold winter months. Below the ground level, plant roots are not under so much stress and looking forward to their mulch layer, along with some fresh compost and downtime from the high water and nutrient demands of the summer.

Some pollinators are lingering that are not ready to give up on the summer and all that pollen still out there, but most are seeking shelter and scoping out their new nests. Garden wildlife, like squirrels and birds, are also looking for food sources during this time of year. An easy way to provide them a food source is to leave withered flowers in your garden for them to eat the seeds. Examples of flowers to leave for them include sunflowers, coneflowers, asters, and cosmos.

During fall season, garden activity really slows down with the day still getting shorter, and many plants are starting their dormancy period to wade through winter and emerge next spring refreshed. Overall, the key to the fall season is preparation.

top These chrysanthemums extend the flowering season when most plants are starting to go dormant. **bottom** This sunflower head provides seeds for birds late in the season when other food sources become scarce.

Seasonal Pruning and Deadheading Examples

WINTER

 Hellebore

 Camellia

 Crocuses

 Pansies

 Asters

SPRING

 Tulips

 Rhododendrons

 Petunias

 Fuchsias

 Crocuses

Hellebores

Camellia

Pansies

SUMMER

 Forsythias

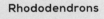 Shasta daisies

 Rhododendrons

 Hydrangeas

 Tulips

 Petunias

 Cosmos

 Fuchsias

FALL

Shasta daisies

Hydrangea

 Chrysanthemums

Asters

Fuchsias

KEY

PRUNING

DEADHEADING

- Pruning occurs only after the plant has flowered, not before. Deadheading can occur while the plant is still actively flowering to encourage more flowers to grow or control diseases.

- Note: These specific plants and flowers are just used as a reference. Their needs may vary from year to year depending on the season or the climate.

getting on a schedule

At this point, you have your new plants planted in your garden. Now you need to get on a regular garden care schedule to make sure your plants stay healthy and get established in their new home. You should make a schedule either on your phone, on your tablet, or even printed out that you can follow and hold yourself accountable to for at least a month or two. Your care schedule will need to become an ongoing habit so you stay on top of your garden chores.

A simple example is to take 10 to 15 minutes each day to tend to your new plants. This could be checking their watering needs looking for weeds in and around your garden beds, or looking for any unknown coloring or growth or weirdness that you don't recognize and want to know more about. The time you spend out in your garden will more than likely change from week to week and month to month, especially when you need to do any monthly or seasonal plant care. Getting on a regular weekly and even daily schedule gives you a sense of accomplishment and keeps your mind at ease. This regular schedule also forces you to get up and outside to interact with your plants. In our sped-up world, we need to unplug regularly to unwind and relax with more natural stimulus around us.

Each month you can mark on your mobile or physical calendar time to get out into your garden. This will also help you plan for any upcoming seasonal cleanups, preparation, mulching, and parties or events you want to host so you can have your plants and garden looking their best for the occasion. This could even be a group event for your family or friends each week or month where you can rotate from garden to garden or duties to duties to help each other and create a sense of community. Just being around and physically touching and handling plants can help with stress, loneliness, anxiety, and depression. Plus, it's fun.

Besides planting, regularly scheduled care will help lengthen these plants' lives.

making renovations and changes to your garden

Each renovation has a silver lining as extra materials are incorporated into your garden with just a little imagination.

After your garden is planted and your plants are established, you might want to update it or add some newer or trendy plants. It's fine to do this, and you shouldn't think you can't. Most gardens go through multiple updates over their life, especially when they have been part of a real estate sale with new owners or when the needs of the owner change for health reasons or a lack of the ability to care for what he or she has.

Any renovation could be for leaf or color, texture, bringing sizes down or lifting up plants, new walkways, clearance around buildings or utilities, or even as your tastes in plants change.

When planning a renovation, be sure to research new plant so that it matches the coldest temperatures in your area, soil conditions and drainage are right, sun exposure is correct, and spacing is right when it reaches its mature size so it doesn't grow into your other plants.

When you have materials or supplies left over from a recent garden project, you can incorporate much of it back into your garden. This is a great zero-waste solution.

For example, concrete blocks and pieces can be used to create new pathways or borders around your garden. Broken clay, stone, or rock containers can be reused in your containers at the bottom to help with drainage. Another example for these broken pieces could be to add them to your garden for a border, art, mulch, or any other creative idea. The sky is the limit. It really is only limited by your creativity. The idea is to reduce waste and reuse as much as you can.

the nature of the garden

Plants, through the four seasons, wake up, grow, flower, and then go dormant to start the whole cycle again. With the changes in temperature, the increase and then decrease of day length throughout a year, along with all the pollinator activity, plants really do have their hands full. Then throw in the whole stay healthy, drink lots of water, and get your vitamins thing! They are living their best life through all kinds of cycles. Being there to help get your plants established and then get them on a schedule can make the biggest difference for their longevity from season to season and year to year.

ECO-FRIENDLY TIP:
LEAVE YOUR LEAVES (AND YOUR STEMS, AND YOUR FLOWERS)

Usually in the late fall, gardeners work hard to pick up and remove their garden debris—including old leaves, stems, and flowers—in advance of the cold, winter months. More recently, a shift has occurred wherein gardeners are realizing the benefits of leaving their gardens a bit more natural. Plant leaves, stems, and some flowers can remain in your garden all winter long, leading to the following benefits:

- Leaves can be used as mulch. They are also great for improving soil structure and nutrient levels.

- Stems left on a plant might not look pretty, but they provide beneficial insect and wildlife habitat.

- Flowers and seed heads left intact can be a great food source for wildlife.

- Branches left on the ground provide nesting and other forms of protection for wildlife.

KEY TAKEAWAYS FROM THIS CHAPTER

Taking care and expanding your garden takes time, patience, and understanding to put it all together.

- Tending to your garden's needs takes place during specific times of the year.

- The sooner you start scheduling your garden care, the sooner your plants will become established, be healthier, and be happier.

DIG DEEPER

To learn even more about zero-waste tips for your leftover garden materials, visit our Bonus Companion Guide to dig deeper into creating a garden pathway using extra project pavers. Check it out in Chapter 7 at spokengarden.com/ftgbonusguide.

chapter

8

Get Out There and Grow

Y ou are part of a community now. You've entered into a network of other hard-working, caring individuals who have developed a love of and passion for gardening at some point in their lives. They were all first-time gardeners once, too, learning, making mistakes, and asking tons of questions. Did they kill plants? Absolutely. Did they know how to prune or water their plants correctly? Not at first. But, guess what? They got outside and tended to their gardens, and they finally grew beautiful plants. But even better than that, throughout the years, their self-confidence in their own ability to be a gardener grew, too. And now, you're a member of this group. It's time for you to get out there and grow.

expectations in the years to come

Change is inevitable in a garden. Luckily, this leads to plenty of opportunities for learning and expanding your skills as a first-time gardener. As you now know, garden care never really ends, and this is your opportunity to continue to grow along with your garden. Getting familiar with different plants that grow in your garden and also in your region takes time. Your plants and flowers will continue to mature throughout each season, providing color, texture, and interest. In the years to come, they'll continue to need your attention. This is the connection we share with our garden.

You will need to replenish your soil with compost, refresh your mulch, prune your plants, deadhead your flowers, renovate your garden beds, and so much more. Eventually, plants such as hostas and daisies will grow so large that they will need to be divided, thus creating new plants to be placed in new homes within your garden or shared with other gardeners.

Critters will continually test and push the limits of your patience by digging in your flower beds, eating your flowering tulip bulbs, or damaging and dislodging your plants. Insect pests will show up even when you do your best to keep them away. Even your garden's watering needs and drainage will change as soil compacts and settles over time.

As you become more familiar with the needs of your garden, you'll be able to anticipate some of these changes over time. Through trial and error, you will continue to hone your skills and prevent problems from occurring. However, nature is unpredictable and oftentimes, even as much as you try to prevent something from happening in your garden, nature will find a way.

As your plants grow and mature, so will your garden care skills.

the wellness connection

As you tend to your plants and flowers, they also care for you in return.

It's a part of the human condition, to be connected to all living organisms in some way. Plants and flowers, with their unique beauty, give us this sense of connection. They offer us comfort, bring us joy and wonder, nourish us, surround us with their scent, and improve our overall sense of well-being. Gardening brings us even closer to understanding nature and helps us grow a deeper connection as we follow the natural cycles of the seasons. We then get to observe how plants react to these seasonal changes as a result.

It is our hope that by reading and applying the information from this book, you have gained a deeper, more connected relationship with nature through your own plants and flowers. All the beauty they provide can only strengthen this connection. You only need to embrace this path and continue to grow along with your plants and flowers.

Your garden journey is already under way, and we are so thankful that we could be a part of it in some way. Happy growing!

ECO-FRIENDLY TIP: YOUR PLANTS AND THE ENVIRONMENT SAY, "THANK YOU!"

You are contributing to a healthier ecosystem just by having a garden and learning how to tend to it. By using certified organic seeds, using less water, finding other uses for your plants, eating your weeds, waiting to clean up your garden, and using sustainable garden products, you are practicing eco-friendly habits. Similar to how plants are eco-friendly by design, you, too, can use only what you need and conserve resources in your garden.

Appendix 1
The First-Time Gardener: Bonus Companion Guide

Throughout this book, each chapter includes bonus material that complements your learning along the way. We created this free material to supplement the concepts you will learn and engage you in extra garden care information in the form of videos, PDF downloads, or audio accompaniments. Since we will be unable to teach you in person while you read, think of this as your personal coaching guide.

To access your free companion guide, visit spokengarden.com/ftgbonusguide and find the corresponding chapter (or chapters) that you need. We hope all the extra resources are helpful!

Visiting this bonus guide is not required by any means, but we strongly urge you to watch, read, and listen to all the free resources we've created for you to help you along your journey to becoming a better gardener. We look forward to seeing you there!

SPOKENGARDEN.COM/FTGBONUSGUIDE

Appendix 2
First-Time Gardener Resources

As a new gardener, you might have specific garden care questions beyond what is presented in this book. We've curated a list of some of our most favorite garden reference books, as well as some of our own popular resources, related to the main garden care questions we receive most often. Our amazing Spoken Garden community challenges us every day to produce better content, whether video, podcast, or written, to provide the best answers to these questions. We hope these are helpful! In addition, after many rounds of discussion, we've created a list of our favorite annuals, perennials, and bulbs for beginning gardeners to grow and tend to in their own gardens. Happy growing!

GARDEN RESOURCES

- *The Horticulture Gardener's Guides: Shrubs* by Andrew McIndoe, 2005

- *The Sunset Western Gardener Book* by Better Homes and Gardens, 2007

- *The American Horticultural Society Encyclopedia of Plants and Flowers*, 2002

PRUNING RESOURCES

- "Thinning vs. Heading Cuts" (spokengarden.com/pruning-basics)

- "Best Pruning Tools" (spokengarden.com/best-pruning-tools)

- "Where to Make Pruning Cuts" (spokengarden.com/pruning-cuts)

MULCHING RESOURCES

- "How to Mulch in 6 Steps" (spokengarden.com/how-to-mulch-6-basic-steps)

- "Top 7 Reasons Mulching Is Beneficial" (spokengarden.com/top-7-reasons-mulching-garden-beneficial)

- "5 Garden Edging Ideas You Can Try Right Now" (spokengarden.com/147-2)

PLANT CARE RESOURCES

- "Summer-Blooming Perennials" (spokengarden.com/summer-blooming-perennials)

- "Shasta Daisy Plant Care" (spokengarden.com/shasta-daisy-plant-profile)

- "How to Create New Plants from Your Existing Garden Plants" (spokengarden.com/51-2)

PEST CONTROL RESOURCES

- "Who's Eating Your Plants and Flowers?" (spokengarden.com/150-2)

- "5 Natural Pest Remedies for Your Garden" (spokengarden.com/5-natural-pest-remedies-for-your-garden)

- "What Plants Are Deer-Resistant?" (spokengarden.com/what-plants-are-deer-resistant)

OUR FAVORITE ANNUALS FOR BEGINNERS

- Petunias
- Cosmos
- Marigolds
- Gerbera daisies
- Sunflowers
- Lobelia
- Coleus
- Impatiens
- Zinnias
- Celosia

OUR FAVORITE PERENNIALS FOR BEGINNERS

- Shasta daisies
- Lavender
- Asters
- Hellebores
- Hostas
- Hydrangeas
- Wild geraniums
- Dianthus
- Campanula
- Sage

OUR FAVORITE BULBS FOR BEGINNERS

- Tulips
- Daffodils
- Alliums
- Crocosmia
- Grape hyacinths (muscari)
- Gladiolus
- Liatris
- Irises
- Crocuses
- Butterfly milkweed

Acknowledgments

We have so many people to thank that it could not possibly fit on this one page, but here goes.

First of all, we have to thank our parents for always believing in us and curating our love of gardening at such an early age.

To Sean's parents, Larry and Sandy: Thank you both for instilling in Sean a hard work ethic, determination, and, Sandy, for the belief that anything is possible as long as you are willing to put in the effort; and, Larry, for never giving up on your dreams or goals. Also, thank you for teaching Sean to always give ideas and people a chance. Sean's approach to everything would not have developed without his mom and dad's extra guidance and patience.

To Allison's mom, Julie: Thank you for teaching Allison the value of hard work, the love of gardening, and appreciation for nature. Oh, and for making her weed the garden when she was younger. To Allison's dad, Roger, who has been gone for so long now but whose garden advice, humor, and good-natured personality pops in Allison's mind every day, thank you.

To our siblings, Brian, Kelcey, and Meghan: You put up with us growing up and have been our biggest supporters ever since. Thank you all for your love, encouragement, and advice throughout the years. We love you!

To Kristi, Hailey, April, Tricia: You guys are the best! Thank you all so much for your love, support, and encouragement throughout this book writing process!

To Roger for always listening and helping Sean when no one else would, and for being a great friend!

To Bri, Kristi, Seren, and Jennie: Thank you ladies for "being a friend" and the love and support you've shown Allison throughout the (many) years!

To Jessica Walliser: Thank you for taking a chance on us and inviting us to author this book. We are so grateful we met you as we all ran to catch the tour bus in Salt Lake, and we truly thank you for inspiring, mentoring, and cheering us all the way to this book's finish line.

To the whole Quarto team, who took our words and photos and turned them into this wonderful book, thank you so much!

And last, but not least, to our *Spoken Garden* community: Thank you for allowing us to teach you and to also learn alongside you. We are forever grateful and dedicate this book to you.

About the Authors

Sean and Allison McManus, the husband-and-wife team behind this book, are garden care educators, podcasters, and new authors. They cofounded the website spokengarden.com to teach others how to become better gardeners and learn how to connect with nature through their shared love of science, gardening, and education.

Both self-professed science nerds, they aim to help others build their confidence and strengthen their plant knowledge with quick, easy garden and plant care tips, tutorials, and how-tos through their YouTube channel, their two podcasts, and their blog. They are members of Garden Communicators International, and this is their first book.

Sean McManus received his master's degree in environmental horticulture from Washington State University. His horticulture training began at an early age as he tended to his family's rhododendron farm in Washington state. He learned how to propagate rhododendrons and studied to take over this family business. This early training sparked his lifelong passion for horticulture which he pursued through two degrees at Washington State University as well as other horticulture, landscaping, and gardening-related job experiences. Sean has over 8 years of experience in industrial garden maintenance and 12+ years of experience operating a private landscape and consulting company.

Allison McManus, a National Board–certified science educator and former middle school science teacher, is the product of two nature-loving parents who instilled in her a deep love and respect for the natural world. From a very young age, she assisted in garden care tasks around the yard when she wasn't stopping to identify birds or butterflies flying around. Always staying in tune with her love of the natural world, she pursued a degree in exercise science at Western Washington University and a master's in teaching degree at City University of Seattle.

The authors currently garden in zone 8b, in Washington state, where they tend to a suburban garden space originally planted by Allison's grandparents. They love growing all kinds of perennials that bloom throughout the year. Over the years, they've renovated, expanded, and removed various portions of the garden, often documented on their YouTube channel. With their combined science knowledge, horticulture training, and general love of teaching others, they're thrilled to help first-time gardeners grow their confidence in garden care.

Follow along with their garden adventures and learn how to become a better gardener at:

Website: spokengarden.com

YouTube: Spoken Garden

Instagram: @spokengarden

Twitter: @SpokenGarden

Pinterest: Spoken Garden

Podcasts

Spoken Garden Podcast: (spokengarden.com/podcast)

DIY Garden Minute Podcast: (spokengarden.com/podcast)

Blog: Spoken Garden (spokengarden.com/blog)

Index